W9-AFM-200

JULIA KRISTEVA

One of the most original thinkers of our time, Julia Kristeva has been a leading force in the fields of literary and cultural studies, psycho-analysis, semiotics, feminist theory, and philosophy. This book gives a lively and lucid account of Kristeva's most important ideas, including her concepts of the semiotic and symbolic, abjection, melancholia, and revolt. Noëlle McAfee provides clear explanations of the more difficult aspects of Kristeva's work, helpfully placing her ideas in the relevant theoretical contexts, and examining their impact on literary studies and critical theory.

Julia Kristeva is the essential guide for readers who are approaching the work of this challenging thinker for the first time and it provides the ideal opportunity for those with more knowledge to re-familiarize themselves with Kristeva's key terms.

Noëlle McAfee is an Associate Professor of Philosophy at the University of Massachusetts Lowell and the Associate Editor of the *Kettering Review*. She is the author of *Habermas, Kristeva, and Citizenship* (2000).

ROUTLEDGE CRITICAL THINKERS

Series Editor: Robert Eaglestone, Royal Holloway, University of London

Routledge Critical Thinkers is a series of accessible introductions to key figures in contemporary critical thought.

With a unique focus on historical and intellectual contexts, each volume examines a key theorist's:

- significance
- motivation
- key ideas and their sources
- impact on other thinkers

Concluding with extensively annotated guides to further reading, *Routledge Critical Thinkers* are the student's passport to today's most exciting critical thought.

Already available:
Roland Barthes by Graham Allen
Jean Baudrillard by Richard J. Lane
Maurice Blanchot by Ullrich Haase and William Large
Judith Butler by Sara Salih
Gilles Deleuze by Claire Colebrook
Jacques Derrida by Nicholas Royle
Michel Foucault by Sara Mills
Sigmund Freud by Pamela Thurschwell
Martin Heidegger by Timothy Clark
Fredric Jameson by Adam Roberts
Jean-François Lyotard by Simon Malpas
Paul de Man by Martin McQuillan
Friedrich Nietzsche by Lee Spinks
Paul Ricoeur by Karl Simms
Edward Said by Bill Ashcroft and Pal Ahluwalia
Gayatri Chakravorty Spivak by Stephen Morton

For further details on this series, see www.literature.routledge.com/rct

JULIA KRISTEVA

Noëlle McAfee

Routledge
Taylor & Francis Group

NEW YORK AND LONDON

First published 2004
Simultaneously published in the UK, USA and Canada by
Routledge
270 Madison Ave, New York, NY 10016
and
Routledge
2 Park Square, Milton Park, Abingdon, Oxon, OX14 4RN

Reprinted 2004, 2005

Transferred to Digital Printing 2007

Routledge is an imprint of the Taylor & Francis Group, an informa business

© 2004 Noëlle McAfee

Typeset in Perpetua by
Florence Production Ltd, Stoodleigh, Devon
Printed and bound in Great Britain by
TJI Digital, Padstow, Cornwall

Library of Congress Cataloging in Publication Data
McAfee, Noëlle, 1960–
    Julia Kristeva/Noëlle McAfee.
      p. cm – (Routledge critical thinkers)
    Includes bibliographical references.
    1. Kristeva, Julia, 1941– –Criticism and interpretation.
    I. Title.   II. Series.
    PN75.K75M38 2003
    801′.85′092–dc21   2003008298

British Library Cataloguing in Publication Data
A catalogue record for this book is available from the
British Library

ISBN 10: 0-415-25008-0 (hbk)   ISBN 13: 978-0-415-25008-5 (hbk)
ISBN 10: 0-415-25009-9 (pbk)   ISBN 13: 978-0-415-25009-2 (pbk)

CONTENTS

SERIES EDITOR'S PREFACE

The books in this series offer introductions to major critical thinkers who have influenced literary studies and the humanities. The *Routledge Critical Thinkers* series provides the books you can turn to first when a new name or concept appears in your studies.

Each book will equip you to approach a key thinker's original texts by explaining her or his key ideas, putting them into context and, perhaps most importantly, showing you why this thinker is considered to be significant. The emphasis is on concise, clearly written guides which do not presuppose a specialist knowledge. Although the focus is on particular figures, the series stresses that no critical thinker ever existed in a vacuum but, instead, emerged from a broader intellectual, cultural and social history. Finally, these books will act as a bridge between you and the thinker's original texts: not replacing them but rather complementing what she or he wrote.

These books are necessary for a number of reasons. In his 1997 autobiography, *Not Entitled*, the literary critic Frank Kermode wrote of a time in the 1960s:

> On beautiful summer lawns, young people lay together all night, recovering from their daytime exertions and listening to a troupe of Balinese musicians. Under their blankets or their sleeping bags, they would chat drowsily about the gurus of the time ... What they repeated was largely hearsay; hence my

lunchtime suggestion, quite impromptu, for a series of short, very cheap books offering authoritative but intelligible introductions to such figures.

There is still a need for 'authoritative and intelligible introductions'. But this series reflects a different world from the 1960s. New thinkers have emerged and the reputations of others have risen and fallen, as new research has developed. New methodologies and challenging ideas have spread through arts and humanities. The study of literature is no longer – if it ever was – simply the study and evaluation of poems, novels and plays. It is also the study of ideas, issues, and difficulties which arise in any literary text and in its interpretation. Other arts and humanities subjects have changed in analogous ways.

With these changes, new problems have emerged. The ideas and issues behind these radical changes in the humanities are often presented without reference to wider contexts or as theories which you can simply 'add on' to the texts you read. Certainly, there's nothing wrong with picking out selected ideas or using what comes to hand – indeed, some thinkers have argued that this is, in fact, all we can do. However, it is sometimes forgotten that each new idea comes from the pattern and development of somebody's thought and it is important to study the range and context of their ideas. Against theories 'floating in space', the *Routledge Critical Thinkers* series places key thinkers and their ideas firmly back in their contexts.

More than this, these books reflect the need to go back to the thinker's own texts and ideas. Every interpretation of an idea, even the most seemingly innocent one, offers its own 'spin', implicitly or explicitly. To read only books on a thinker, rather than texts by that thinker, is to deny yourself a chance of making up your own mind. Sometimes what makes a significant figure's work hard to approach is not so much its style or content as the feeling of not knowing where to start. The purpose of these books is to give you a 'way in' by offering an accessible overview of these thinkers' ideas and works and by guiding your further reading, starting with each thinker's own texts. To use a metaphor from the philosopher Ludwig Wittgenstein (1889–1951), these books are ladders, to be thrown away after you have climbed to the next level. Not only, then, do they equip you to approach new ideas, but also they empower you, by leading you back to the theorist's own texts and encouraging you to develop your own informed opinions.

Finally, these books are necessary because, just as intellectual needs have changed, the education systems around the world – the contexts in which introductory books are usually read – have changed radically, too. What was suitable for the minority higher education system of the 1960s is not suitable for the larger, wider, more diverse, high technology education systems of the twenty-first century. These changes call not just for new, up-to-date, introductions but new methods of presentation. The presentational aspects of *Routledge Critical Thinkers* have been developed with today's students in mind.

Each book in the series has a similar structure. They begin with a section offering an overview of the life and ideas of each thinker and explain why she or he is important. The central section of each book discusses the thinker's key ideas, their context, evolution and reception. Each book concludes with a survey of the thinker's impact, outlining how their ideas have been taken up and developed by others. In addition, there is a detailed final section suggesting and describing books for further reading. This is not a 'tacked-on' section but an integral part of each volume. In the first part of this section you will find brief descriptions of the thinker's key works: following this, information on the most useful critical works and, in some cases, on relevant websites. This section will guide you in your reading, enabling you to follow your interests and develop your own projects. Throughout each book, references are given in what is known as the Harvard system (the author and the date of a work cited are given in the text and you can look up the full details in the bibliography at the back). This offers a lot of information in very little space. The books also explain technical terms and use boxes to describe events or ideas in more detail, away from the main emphasis of the discussion. Boxes are also used at times to highlight definitions of terms frequently used or coined by a thinker. In this way, the boxes serve as a kind of glossary, easily identified when flicking through the book.

The thinkers in the series are 'critical' for three reasons. First, they are examined in the light of subjects which involve criticism: principally literary studies or English and cultural studies, but also other disciplines which rely on the criticism of books, ideas, theories and unquestioned assumptions. Second, they are critical because studying their work will provide you with a 'tool kit' for your own informed critical reading and thought, which will make you critical. Third, these thinkers are critical because they are crucially important: they deal with ideas and questions which can overturn conventional understandings of the world, of texts, of everything we take for granted, leaving us with a deeper understanding of what we already knew and with new ideas.

No introduction can tell you everything. However, by offering a way into critical thinking, this series hopes to begin to engage you in an activity which is productive, constructive and potentially life-changing.

ACKNOWLEDGMENTS

I am deeply indebted to Bob Eaglestone and Liz Thompson for their guidance and patience throughout the writing of this book. I would also like to thank the anonymous readers for their suggestions, which made this a better book. Thanks also go to Tina Chanter, Kelly Oliver, and Ewa Ziarek for their thoughts on Kristeva's influence, as well as to my colleagues in the philosophy department at the University of Massachusetts Lowell: Bob Innis, Whit Kaufman, Gene Mellican, and Chris Smith. Finally, I thank Eliza, Guthrie, and David Armstrong for the nourishment we call home. I dedicate this book to Eliza.

A portion of Chapter 5 first appeared in *Philosophy Today* 44, SPEP Supplement 2000: 77–83. For details see McAfee (2000a) in the Works Cited section.

WHY KRISTEVA?

Julia Kristeva is one of the most original thinkers of our time. She is one of very few philosophers for whom the speaking being becomes a crucial constellation for understanding oral and written literature, politics and national identity, sexuality, culture, and nature. Where other thinkers might see these fields as separate domains, Kristeva shows that the speaking being is "a strange fold" between them all – a place where inner drives are discharged into language, where sexuality interplays with thought, where the body and culture meet. Under Kristeva's gaze, no border stands untouched by the forces on either side of it. To live is to be in a state of change, to be nearly under siege from a variety of forces. This is one reason why much of her work focuses on the "borderline" patients who frequent psychoanalysts' couches. They manifest the very same conditions we all do when the affective dimensions of living disrupt our even mental keel. Kristeva's work shows how what we call subjectivity is always a tenuous accomplishment, a dynamic process never completed.

Kristeva and her cohorts offer the term *subjectivity* as an alternative to the conventional understanding of "self," a term used to designate a being who is fully aware of her own intentions, fully able to act as an autonomous being in the world, and guided by her reason and intellect. Conventionally, "the self" uses language as a tool to convey ideas. She says what she means and intends what she says. This self is, ideally, master of her own being, subject to no one. The term *subjectivity* suggests something altogether different. Those who proffer this term think that the Western philosophic tradition is deeply mistaken about how human beings come to be who they are. First, persons are subject to all kinds of phenomena: their culture, history, context, relationships, and language. These phenomena profoundly shape how people come to be. Thus, persons are better understood as subjects not selves. Second, subjects are not fully aware of all the phenomena that shape them. There is even a dimension of their own being that is inaccessible, a dimension that goes by the name, "the unconscious." The unconscious is the domain of desires, tensions, energy, and repressions that is not present in consciousness. Therefore, the experience of subjectivity is not that of coming to awareness as a "self," but of having an identity wrought in ways often unbeknownst to the subject herself. And finally, the term *subjectivity* better explains people's relationship to language. Instead of seeing language as a tool used by selves, those who use the term *subjectivity* understand that language helps produce subjects.

As I will discuss in these pages, Kristeva is part of a philosophic tradition that takes this notion of subjectivity as a starting point. This tradition can be traced back to the early nineteenth century, certainly to the work of the German philosopher, Georg Wilhelm Friedrich Hegel (1770–1831), who argued persuasively against the notion of the autonomous, self-conscious individual. Later in the nineteenth century, the German philosopher, Friedrich Wilhelm Nietzsche (1844–1900), advanced this critique, arguing that the notion of the self as a unified and rational being was an illusion inimical to life itself. In the twentieth century, a series of philosophers in France took Hegel's and Nietzsche's insights further, and we can locate Kristeva as part of this philosophical trajectory. In the 1960s and 1970s, Kristeva was one of the first thinkers to usher in "post-structuralism," an intellectual movement that has had enormous impact in philosophical and literary circles. (I discuss this movement later in this introduction.) What sets Kristeva apart – and so what answers the title of this introduction – is that she has come up with very powerful tools for understanding how language produces speaking beings who emerge in that fold between language and culture. She offers a sustained and nuanced understanding of how subjectivity is produced; how language actually operates when people speak, write, and create; and how beings who are already at odds with "the other" within might come to terms with the others in their midst.

At first glance, Julia Kristeva seems to be of two minds about things. She revels in the revolutionary potential of poetic language, yet she is careful not to take its "asymbolia" (loss of meaning) too far. She conjures up a radically new understanding of maternal, "heretical" (that is, subversive to the established order, unorthodox) ethics, yet she does so within a discourse (psychoanalysis) that is steeped in paternal authority. She documents how people are both fascinated and repelled by the foreigners in their midst, but she sees this attitude toward "foreignness" as a necessary and constitutive feature of our self-identity. She points to the importance of biological drives and energy, but notes that they can only be apprehended via our language and culture. She writes with feminist intent, but she is critical of the movement known as feminism.

No wonder, then, that Kristeva has been castigated by critics from all sides – and that her work has been so often misunderstood. (In the 1980s and 1990s several Anglo-American feminist philosophers launched criticisms against Kristeva's work because of its supposedly anti-feminist adherence to psychoanalytic theory. See my annotation of a book by Nancy Fraser and Sandra Bartky in the "Further reading" section at the end of this book.) Her various styles of writing do not help. Her earliest works are noted for their highly theoretical, abstract, and nearly turgid prose (namely her early book, *Revolution in Poetic Language* (1974)), and some of her later writings are marked by a difficulty of another sort: a kind of poetic inventiveness and multiplicity (such as in "Stabat Mater" (1977) and *Powers of Horror* (1980)).

Still one ignores or writes off Kristeva at one's own intellectual risk. She is not, in fact, of two minds about things. The seeming discrepancies in her thought are, in actuality, manifestations of her attempt to help us all find a balance between the "excesses" of nature and the constraints of culture, even as she tries to unravel the polarity I am now invoking between these two domains. As someone bringing together insights from fields as far flung as psychoanalytic theory, religious scholarship, avant-garde literature, and philosophy, Kristeva is one of the most original and influential thinkers of our time. She has changed the terrain in literary criticism, psychoanalytic theory, linguistics, and feminist philosophy. She has also ventured into political theory and fiction writing. She is one of the most popular intellectuals in Paris (regularly appearing on television and continuing to publish new books) and a regular subject of panels at academic conferences in the United States, England, and Australia.

LIFE AND CONTEXTS

Kristeva was born in Bulgaria in 1941. Her father, trained as a doctor, worked as an accountant for the Church and consequently was not in the good graces of the reigning Communist Party (the Communists being avowedly atheist). As a result, the young Julia Kristeva was not allowed the perks of membership of the Communist Party – she wasn't allowed to attend the government-sponsored French schools or to carry the flag in parades, as the best students usually did. Her father sent her and her sister to a school run by Dominican nuns, where she was able to study in French and flourish as a student. Studying in the Eastern Bloc, Kristeva came to know the work of the Russian Formalists (as discussed in Chapter 2, a group of linguists who identified the structures of language in the early decades of the twentieth century), as well as the work of the Eastern European thinker, Mikhail Bakhtin (1895–1975), one of the leading social and literary philosophers of the twentieth century, who was still unknown in the West. When she was writing her doctoral thesis on the *nouveau roman* (a new style of novel penned in France after World War II by a group of avant-garde writers), she learned of a scholarship the French government was offering to qualified young people wanting to study in France. Just before Christmas of 1965, when the diehard communist director of her college was in Moscow, her thesis director took her to the French embassy, where she wrote and passed the exam for the scholarship to study in France. The scholarship money would come through by the end of January, but Kristeva was worried that the college's director would return and forbid her from leaving. So she left immediately with just five dollars in her pocket.

Arriving in Paris on Christmas Eve, she chanced to meet a Bulgarian journalist with whom she stayed until her scholarship money came through. Then, less by happenstance, she fell in with a new generation of intellectuals:

> At the end of '65, I landed at Lucien Goldmann's and Roland Barthes' doors at the [L'ecole Pratique des] Hautes etudes. Lucien Goldmann welcomed me to

his seminar on the "sociology of the novel" with fraternal distraction, convinced that I was a congenital Marxist, since I came from Eastern Europe.

(Kristeva 1997: 7–8)

A fellow exile and literary theorist, Goldmann (1913–1970), who was from Romania, helped her immeasurably, she says: "It was a kind of help that only those exiled from any country know how to give" (Kristeva 1997: 8). Subsequently, Goldmann directed her thesis on the origins of the novel. As for the literary theorist, Roland Barthes (1915–1980): "the teaching of Roland Barthes attracted me because of its capacity to make formalism, which I had found reductive, extremely appealing" (Kristeva 1997: 8). In these circles she also came to meet the anthropologist, Claude Lévi-Strauss (1908–), the linguist, Émile Benveniste (1902–1976), the psychoanalyst, Jacques Lacan (1901–1981), the philosopher, Michel Foucault (1926–1984), and others working variously in the vein known as structuralism, an intellectual approach that sought to locate and analyze structures in everything from kinship networks to language to the unconscious.

With her keen intellect and her background in Russian Formalism (one of the original manifestations of structuralism, which I explain further in Chapter 2), Kristeva immediately made a name for herself. The first impression she made was in a paper she presented. "I introduced someone who was unknown at the time in the West: Mikhail Bakhtin, and his notions of inter-textuality, of dialogue, and of the carnivalization of the novel" (Kuprel 2000). As she soon wrote in her first book, *Semiotiké: Recherches pour une sémanalyse* (*Semiotics: Investigations for Semanalysis*):

Writer as well as "scholar," Bakhtin was one of the first to replace the static hewing out of texts with a model where literary structure does not simply *exist* but is generated in relation to *another* structure. What allows a dynamic dimension to structuralism is his conception of the "literary word" as an *intersection of textual surfaces* rather than a *point* (a fixed meaning), as a dialogue among several writings: that of the writer, the addressee (or the character), and the contemporary or earlier cultural context.

(Kristeva 1980: 64–65)

Such a "literary word" par excellence is the poetic word, Kristeva explains, and its logic is found in what Bakhtin calls *carnival*: "Carnivalesque discourse breaks through the laws of a language censored by grammar and semantics and, at the same time, is a social and political protest" (Kristeva 1980: 65). Her explanation and development of Bakhtin was so well received that she immediately got a job offer, she says, to teach in the United States. She turned it down because of the war the United States was carrying out in Vietnam, which she opposed (Guberman 1996: 5). She joined what was called the *Tel Quel* (or "Such as it is") group, the editorial collective of the journal by the same name. One of the group's members was the novelist, Philippe Sollers, whom she soon married and with whom she had a son in the mid-1970s.

The mid-1960s were heady times to be in Paris, especially in the four streets of the Left Bank that Kristeva now called home. As part of the *Tel Quel* group, Kristeva later told an interviewer, "we would have deep discussions until all hours of the night at 55 Rue de Rennes, where many people would come to discuss philosophy and literature. The animated intellectual world convinced me that I could live abroad" (Guberman 1996: 6). Intellectually and politically – not to mention sexually – revolution was in the air. Intellectually, the revolution was aimed at infusing theory with the dynamics of history, change, and, especially for Kristeva, the living, breathing "speaking being."

> For us, structuralism ... was already accepted knowledge. To simplify, this meant that one should no longer lose sight of the real constraints, "material," as we used to say, of what had previously and trivially been viewed as "form." For us, the logic of this formal reality constituted the very meaning of phenomena or events that then became structures (from kinship to literary texts) and thus achieved intelligibility without necessarily relying on "external factors." From the outset, however, our task was to take this acquired knowledge and immediately do something else.
>
> (Kristeva 1997: 9)

Kristeva and others in her circle of intellectuals built upon the insights of structuralism to "do something else" – something they thought was simultaneously political and philosophical, for they believed that any linguistic intervention was also a political one; namely, they chose to look for the dynamic, changing aspects of systems. Where structuralism looked at systems synchronically (in a snapshot of time), post-structuralism looked at systems diachronically, through time, as events or processes. "I was one of the people who helped to formulate a type of post-structuralism," she later told an interviewer, using the phrase "post-structuralism" as a modification of the familiar "structuralism." Post-structuralism was new in that it brought in history, time, process, change, event: it broke up the static way that structuralists understood things. "My position was that mere structure was not sufficient to understand the world of meaning in literature and other human behaviors. Two more elements were necessary: history and the speaking subject" (Kuprel 2000). Along these lines, Kristeva and other post-structuralists helped push aside the notion of "the self" that I discussed at the outset with the concept of "speaking beings," who are subject to the vicissitudes of history, language, and other shaping forces. Kristeva's contribution is often overshadowed by one of the more famous members of her circle, Jacques Derrida (1930–), who took the account of language offered by Ferdinand de Saussure (1857–1913), the Swiss linguist and founder of structural linguistics, and created a way to "deconstruct" language and structuralism itself. But, where Derrida was concerned with deconstructing structuralism, Kristeva thought it essential to "'dynamize' the structure by taking into consideration the speaking subject and its unconscious experience on the one hand and, on the other, the pressures of other social structures" (Kristeva 1997: 9).

To this end, after completing her thesis on the origin of the novel, she set to work on what may be her most important book, *La révolution du langage poétique* (1974), a part of which was translated ten years later as *Revolution in Poetic Language*. The "revolution" she describes is the one performed by avant-garde writers, such as the French poets, Stéphane Mallarmé (1842–1898) and Comte de Lautréamont (1846–1870), whose poetic language calls up an aspect of the signifying process that destabilizes the symbolic, logical, and orderly aspects of signifying. I will go into the details in the next chapter, but suffice it to say for now that Kristeva's attention to poetic language showed how dynamic subjectivity really is.

As for the political revolution, by May 1968 students and workers in Paris had shut down the city with a massive strike. May '68 saw similar rebellions throughout the world, but in Paris the confluence of workers, students, and intellectuals working to change the world made the dream seem almost possible. But then it all collapsed. And it turned out that one of the leading betrayers of the cause was none other than the French Communist Party, a political party with which many left intellectuals had felt common cause. The budding revolutionaries were deeply chagrined.

Still the *Tel Quel* group carried on and, in 1974, under the spell of Maoism (the approach to communism developed by China's communist leader, Mao Zedong (1893–1976)), some of its members, Kristeva included, made a three-week trip to China to see how, as one journalist has put it, "socialism could marry with an ancient and subtle culture, one they considered comparable to France" (Hughes-Hallett 1992). They were disappointed, to say the least: "I myself was alarmed by the profound, unflagging, sly presence of the Soviet model," Kristeva later wrote in a memoir, "the only sign of the twentieth century in this land of peasants, and all the more evident because [this model] was violently resisted" (Kristeva 1997: 19). Instead of the ethereal socialism they sought, they found the signs of the imminence of Soviet-style communism, which Kristeva had already quit in Bulgaria. The trip to China, Kristeva later wrote, marked her "farewell to politics" (Kristeva 1997: 19). But the trip was fruitful in an unexpected way: what she saw led her to write what she has called "an awkward book," *Des Chinoises* (1974), a portion of which was translated into English as "About Chinese Women" (and published in Toril Moi's *The Kristeva Reader* (Kristeva 1986)). In this book, she has said recently, perhaps in response to critics who say she was being "orientalist," that is, portraying the East as the inferior other, she "tried to convey the strangeness of China and to explain the fascination we Occidentals feel for it, a fascination unquestionably involved with our own strange, foreign, feminine, psychotic aspects" (Kristeva 1997: 19; also Oliver 1993: 150–163).

China gave Kristeva a glimpse of the internal territory she needed to encounter. Upon her return to Paris, she went into psychoanalysis, a way to educate herself about "the only continent we had never left: internal experience" (Kristeva 1997: 19):

> The psychoanalytic experience struck me as the only one in which the wildness of the speaking being, and of language, can be heard. Political adventures, against the background of desire and hate that analysis openly unveils, appeared to me the way distance changes them: like a power of horror, like abjection.

> (ibid.)

Her subsequent theoretical works reflected this new interest. Where her writing of the 1960s and 1970s focused on semiotics and language, her texts of the 1980s take the psychoanalytic experience of the speaking subject as their point of departure. Later she calls what she was doing "politics at the micro level," at the level of the individual. She even suggests that psychoanalysis might be a political remedy for the xenophobia that leads to political repression worldwide (Kristeva 1991).

In the 1990s, Kristeva's writings took two new turns. First, she re-entered the (macro)political scene with a few essays in politics, including *Lettre ouverte à Harlem Désir* (1990), translated as "Open Letter to Harlem Désir" and published in *Nations without Nationalism* (1993). Second, she turned to fiction, with the publication of books translated as *The Samurai* (1992) and *The Old Man and the Wolves* (1994), as well as the detective novel, *Possessions* (1996).

Kristeva is currently the Director of the École Doctorale: Langues, Littératures et Civilisations at the Université de Paris VII. She is a practicing psychoanalyst and has served as a visiting professor at Columbia University in New York and at the University of Toronto. She continues to be a prolific writer, with her most recent work on the writings and lives of the German-American theorist, Hannah Arendt, the psychoanalyst, Melanie Klein, and the French writer, Colette.

THIS BOOK

The core of this book examines Kristeva's key ideas. Kristeva's post-structuralism has focused on speaking subjects – human beings who signify and are constituted through their signifying practices. This makes it impossible to study her theory of language apart from her theory of subjectivity. This difficulty presents a slight challenge in writing a book explaining Kristeva's project and her key terms; thus the themes of the various chapters of this book will slip into one another.

The first chapter will cover the key points in her groundbreaking text, *Revolution in Poetic Language*, which are still extremely important aspects of her work, namely her theory of language and what she calls the semiotic and the symbolic. Chapter 2 will turn to the theory of subjectivity that underlies her theory of language and the way in which this subjectivity is always "in process." Chapter 3 looks at the way this subjectivity can founder, how its borders can fail to hold, and at the promise Kristeva finds for developing a new psychic space. Chapter 4 gives an overview of her work on depression and melancholia. Chapters 5 and 6 turn to her views on maternity, female sexuality, and feminism, including discussions of other feminists' criticisms of her work. Chapter 7 discusses Kristeva's notion of the importance of revolt in language, politics, and subjectivity. Finally, "After Kristeva," discusses the impact that Kristeva's ideas have had in literary studies, continental philosophy, feminist theory, and political theory. To help those approaching Kristeva's texts for the first time, a final section provides an annotated bibliography of Kristeva's main books, as well as an overview of some of the best books and web sites available on Kristeva.

KEY IDEAS

1

SEMIOTIC AND SYMBOLIC

This chapter covers key points in Kristeva's theory of language, including her notions of the *chora*, the semiotic, and the symbolic. She first articulated these in her early books, primarily in *Semiotiké: Recherches pour une sémanalyse* of 1969, of which only two chapters have been translated into English, and her groundbreaking text of 1974, *La révolution du langage poétique*, a third of which was translated into English and published in 1984 as *Revolution in Poetic Language*. The English-language version of *Revolution* contains the theoretical portion of the text and omits its critical application to the literary works of avant-garde writers. The thesis of *Revolution in Poetic Language* is this: the works of literary avant-garde writers produce a "revolution in poetic language." That is, they contain elements that "shatter" the way we think that texts are meaningful. Meaning is not made just denotatively, with words denoting thoughts or things. Meaning is made in large part by the poetic and affective aspects of texts as well. This revolution is not limited to the language of artists, but is present in ways that ordinary human beings try to express themselves. All our attempts to use language neatly, clearly, and in an orderly way are handmaidens of our attempts to be neat, clearly demarcated, orderly subjects. But such attempts are continuously disrupted by certain elements of our signifying practice.

Throughout her writing, Julia Kristeva focuses on "speaking beings" – those who not only use language but are constituted through their use of language. Kristeva describes language as the discursive or signifying system in which "the speaking subject *makes* and *unmakes* himself" (Kristeva 1989b: 265, 272). In Kristeva's view, as the philosopher Kelly Oliver has noted, "any theory of language is a theory of the subject" (see Oliver's introduction to Kristeva (1997: xviii)). Thus Kristeva folds two huge areas of inquiry – subjectivity and language – into one. This twofold aspect of her work makes writing this book on Kristeva difficult. I cannot begin to address her theory of language without also discussing her theory of subjectivity. Nor can I do the opposite. As we'll see, we cannot set her views on language apart from the beings who use it. In Kristeva's view, language is not a tool that we pick up from time to time. And there is not a speaking being to consider unless this being is speaking or using language in some way. To make matters all the more complex, we are engaging in this work using language ourselves.

THE SIGNIFYING PROCESS

One way to approach Kristeva's theory of language is to compare it to the other theories that were accepted when she wrote *Revolution in Poetic Language*. Kristeva's view of them is rather harsh: "Our philosophies of language, embodiments of the Idea, are nothing more than the thoughts of archivists, archaeologists, and necrophiliacs" (Kristeva 1984: 13). In other words, most non-post-structuralist theories of language treat language as a dead artifact, something that can be cataloged, archived, entombed – a formal object of study. They do this in keeping with larger socio-economic forces, namely capitalism, which treat people and their languages as isolable, static entities. In so doing, they deny the dynamic processes in which people generate meaning and experience.

Along with others in her circle on the Left Bank, Kristeva entered the field to change all that. Instead of treating language as a separate, static entity, Kristeva has seen it as part of a dynamic *signifying process*. Kristeva never explicitly defines this key term, but she seems to use it to mean the ways in which bodily drives and energy are expressed, literally discharged through our use of language, and how our signifying practices shape our subjectivity and experience: "linguistic changes constitute changes in the *status of the subject* – his relation to the body, to others, and to objects" (Kristeva 1984: 15). Kelly Oliver describes Kristeva's view of signifying practice this way:

> Instead of lamenting what is lost, absent, or impossible in language, Kristeva marvels at this other realm [bodily experience] that makes its way into language. The force of language is [a] living driving force transferred into language. Signification is like a transfusion of the living body into language.
>
> (Oliver 1997: xx)

So we should not study language apart from "the subject of enunciation," "the subject who 'means,'" or, to put it more plainly, the person who is talking or writing and trying to express something. For this speaking being's own living energy infuses meaning into language. The best example of this phenomenon is a negative one: think of what it is like to talk with someone who lacks what psychiatrists call "affect," that is, evident feeling or emotion. This is sometimes the case with someone who is severely depressed. Such a person's speech may be devoid of the usual rhythms and modulations that infuse speech with meaning. He or she speaks with no enthusiasm and seems to be nearly absent from the conversation. A listener would take away very little from the words that are uttered, for they do not seem to signify anything real or vital.

Interestingly, our everyday uses of language in social settings generally operate by trying to contain the "excesses" of language, that is, the potentially explosive ways in which signifying practices exceed the subject and his or her communicative structures (Kristeva 1984: 16). Some such excesses have been sanctioned in the arts, religion, and rites – realms in which passions that might disrupt the social order are channeled. But in "polite society" we are expected to "contain ourselves." For most of us, we have to find a path between the two poles of language, devoid of affect and expressions that overwhelm order.

TWO MODES OF SIGNIFICATION

In fact, when we attend to language within the signifying process, Kristeva says, we may notice two ways or modes in which it operates: (1) as an expression of clear and orderly meaning; and (2) as an evocation of feeling or, more pointedly, a discharge of the subject's energy and drives. In other words, we may find ourselves using certain words because they get something across clearly or because they express some feeling, desire, or unconscious drive. The words she uses for these modes are, respectively, symbolic and semiotic. These terms draw on a rich background of linguistic and psychoanalytic theory, to which I will turn shortly. First, notice the following passage from Molly's soliloquy at the end of James Joyce's *Ulysses*:

> the sun shines for you he said the day we were lying among the rhododendrons on Howth head in the grey tweed suit and his straw hat the day I got him to propose to me yes first I gave him the bit of seedcake out of my mouth and it was leapyear like now yes 16 years ago my God after that long kiss I near lost my breath yes he said I was a flower of the mountain yes so we are flowers all a womans body yes that was one true thing he said in his life and the sun shines for you today yes that was why I liked him because I saw he understood or felt what a woman is and I knew I could always get round him and I gave him all the pleasure I could leading him on till he asked me to say yes.
>
> (643)

Believe it or not, I've selected one of the more coherent passages from Molly's soliloquy. It expresses meaning in both modes that Kristeva discusses: (1) symbolically, i.e. through the use of logical terms; and (2) semiotically, through a breathless (punctuation-less) flow of words that are more emotive than logical. Clearly this passage partakes of the second mode more than the first, at least in so far as Joyce's semiotic signification helped produce Molly's stream of consciousness. Molly shifts back and forth in time and perspective. We get a keen sense of Molly's *jouissance* (one of Kristeva's favorite terms to signify both erotic and psychic pleasure). We read Molly's uncensored thoughts in her stream-of-consciousness recollections. This is an important part of semiotic signification: Molly's prose comes forth almost unbidden from a wellspring of internal desires and drives, or at least Joyce's writing seems to do so.

To help understand the distinction between semiotic and symbolic, the reader could imagine mapping that dichotomy onto more familiar dichotomies: such as the distinctions between nature and culture, between body and mind, between the unconscious and consciousness, and between feeling and reason. In the history of Western thought, these dichotomies are usually taken to be extreme opposites: either one

THE SEMIOTIC AND THE SYMBOLIC

In Kristeva's theory, the signifying process has two modes: the semiotic and the symbolic. The semiotic (*le sémiotique*, not *la sémiotique*, which means semiotics, the study of signs) is the extra-verbal way in which bodily energy and affects make their way into language. The semiotic includes both the subject's drives and articulations. While the semiotic may be expressed verbally, it is not subject to regular rules of syntax. Conversely, the symbolic is a way of signifying that depends on language as a sign system complete with its grammar and syntax (Kristeva 1984: 27). The symbolic is a mode of signifying in which speaking beings attempt to express meaning with as little ambiguity as possible. The expressions of scientists and logicians are paradigmatic examples of people trying to use symbolic language, whereas expressions found in music, dance, and poetry exemplify the semiotic. The semiotic could be seen as the modes of expression that originate in the unconscious whereas the symbolic could be seen as the conscious way a person tries to express using a stable sign system (whether written, spoken, or gestured with sign language). The two modes, however, are not completely separate: we use symbolic modes of signifying to state a position, but this position can be destabilized or unsettled by semiotic drives and articulations.

is a savage brute or a civilized human being; either one is acting out of lust or using one's head; either one is driven by emotion or steered by reason. The difference with Kristeva's use of these kinds of polarities is that the former pole (semiotic/nature/body/unconscious, etc.) always makes itself felt – is discharged – into the latter (symbolic/culture/mind/consciousness). Instead of holding to the dualistic thinking of the West, Kristeva is showing how the poles of these dichotomies are intertwined.

In a certain respect it may seem that the symbolic and the semiotic modes of signification are at odds with each other. This may be so, but certainly it is also true that the combination of Joyce's symbolic mode of signification (his words with clearly demarcated meaning) and his semiotic mode (a syntax that undercuts order) together signify something more than the sum of the parts of Molly's words. We have here neither pure logic nor pure music. What we have is a symbolic mode of signification (the words in whatever semantic order they are given) that is energized by a semiotic dimension. Molly says "that after that long kiss I nearly lost my breath" and the words are energized by the breathless semiotic rhythm of the text. This is Kristeva's point: the symbolic mode of signification is meaningful because of the way the semiotic energizes it. If it weren't for the bodily energy that speaking beings bring to (and put into) language, language would have little if any meaning for us.

THE SEMIOTIC *CHORA*

Well before the subject begins to use language symbolically – through the use of symbols, grammar, and syntax – she expresses herself with various intonations and gestures. Think of a baby's coos and babbles or her imitations of the rhythms of her parents' speech. This kind of signifying is part of what Kristeva calls the semiotic: "We understand the term 'semiotic' in its Greek sense: σημεῖον=distinctive mark, trace, index, precursory sign, proof, engraved or written sign, imprint, trace, figuration" (Kristeva 1984: 25). The semiotic aspect of signification signifies what is "below the surface" of the speaking being:

> Discrete quantities of energy move through the body of the subject who is not yet constituted as such and, in the course of his development, they are arranged according to the various constraints imposed on this body – always already involved in a semiotic process – by family and social structures. In this way the drives, which are "energy" charges as well as "psychical" marks, articulate what we call a *chora*: a nonexpressive totality formed by the drives and their stases in a motility that is as full of movement as it is regulated.
>
> (Kristeva 1984: 25)

By *motile*, Kristeva means the quality of exhibiting or being capable of spontaneous movement.

Kristeva borrows the term *chora* from Plato's *Timaeus* to "denote an essentially mobile and extremely provisional articulation constituted by movements and their ephemeral stases" (1984: 25). But even with Plato on her side, Kristeva's notion of the *chora* is extremely hazy: the *chora* is often translated as womb or receptacle, but Kristeva doesn't seem to mean that it is just a space; she says it is an articulation, a rhythm, but one that precedes language. Kristeva's ambiguity can be traced back to the *Timaeus* itself. Plato offered the terms *receptacle* and *chora* to

THE *CHORA*

The Greek philosopher Plato (427–347 BC) coined a term on which Kristeva draws. In one of his works titled the *Timaeus*, Plato gives his own explanation for how the universe was created. In the process he uses the word *chora*, meaning both receptacle and nurse, that is, the container and the producer, of what the universe is before and as anything exists. With the term *chora*, Kristeva describes how an infant's psychic environment is oriented to its mother's body: "Plato's *Timaeus* speaks of a chora, receptacle, unnamable, improbable, hybrid, anterior to naming, to the One, to the father, and consequently, maternally connoted to such an extent that it merits 'not even the rank of syllable'" (1980: 133). Plato meant by the term the original space or receptacle of the universe, but Kristeva seems to have something in mind that belongs to each person in particular before he or she develops clear borders of his or her own personal identity. In this early psychic space, the infant experiences a wealth of drives (feelings, instincts, etc.) that could be extremely disorienting and destructive were it not for the infant's relation with his or her mother's body. An infant's tactile relation with its mother's body provides an orientation for the infant's drives. Kristeva often uses the term *chora* in conjunction with the term *semiotic*: her phrase "the semiotic *chora*" reminds the reader that the *chora* is the space in which the meaning that is produced is semiotic: the echolalis, glossolalias, rhythms, and intonations of an infant who does not yet know how to use language to refer to objects, or of a psychotic who has lost the ability to use language in a properly meaningful way. The semiotic *chora* may also make itself felt in symbolic communication.

describe a space in which the universe comes to reside. The *chora* is a space

> which exists always and cannot be destroyed. It provides a fixed site for all things that come to be. It is itself apprehended by a kind of bastard reasoning that does not involve sense perception, and it is hardly even an object of conviction. We look at it as in a dream when we say that everything that exists must of necessity be somewhere, in some place and occupying some space.
>
> (*Timaeus*: 52b–c)

Plato's musings about the origins of the universe are ones we might adopt today, using a more modern vocabulary. In addition to asking

"What was there before the big bang?" and "Where did the universe come from?" we might ask "Where is this universe?" or "In what space did the universe come to be?" This account makes it seem that the receptacle is merely a passive space, but this is not the case: the *chora* is not just a "receptacle of all becoming," it is "its wetnurse, as it were" (*Timaeus*: 49b). As a receptacle, Plato likens the *chora* to a mother (as a space that receives and allows something to flourish). But this "mother" has no qualities of its own; it fully takes on the imprint of whatever fills it — and derives its powers from what fills it:

> Now as the wetnurse of becoming turns watery and fiery and receives that character of earth and air, and as it acquires all the properties that come with these characters, it takes on a variety of visible aspects, but because it is filled with powers that are neither similar nor evenly balanced, no part of it is in balance. It sways irregularly in every direction as it is shaken by those things, and being set in motion it in turn shakes them. And as they are moved, they drift continually, some in one direction and others in others, separating from one another. They are winnowed out, as it were.
>
> (*Timaeus*: 52d–53a)

Kristeva says she is only "borrowing" Plato's term; she doesn't claim to be adopting it wholesale. She downplays the Platonic view of the *chora* as amorphous, formless, and completely malleable to whatever fills it, in favor of Plato's view of the *chora* as the wetnurse of becoming. Kristeva emphasizes the *chora*'s motility, which, as I mentioned above, means exhibiting or being capable of spontaneous movement. Kristeva wants to see the *chora* as capable of generating (not just receiving) energy — the energy which helps fuel the signifying process. She finds, "in this rhythmic space, which has no thesis and no position, the process by which signifiance is constituted" (Kristeva 1984: 26).

At first the child is immersed in this semiotic *chora*. It expresses itself in the baby talk of coos and babbles. It uses sounds and gestures to express itself and to discharge energy. It does not yet grasp that an utterance can express something — or that there is any salient difference between various things and itself. Yet, as this awareness occurs and deepens, everything changes. The child begins to realize that language can be used to point out objects and events. At the same time, the child begins to realize its own difference from its surroundings. It becomes aware of the difference between self (subject) and other (object). It comprehends that language can point to things outside itself, that it is potentially referential. Kristeva calls this the thetic break. An observer can see this at work well before a child begins to speak in sentences. Even sounds that at first seem semiotic – e.g. imitating the "woof-woof" of a dog – are first steps into the act of making propositions, thus first steps into the symbolic. The child has identified a dog as something separate from itself. This act "constitutes an *attribution*, which is to say, a positing of identity or difference." It "represents the nucleus of judgment or proposition" (Kristeva 1984: 43).

Kristeva borrows the notion of the thetic from Edmund Husserl (1859–1938), the German philosopher who founded the type of philosophy called phenomenology (roughly, the study of appearances and consciousness); but she develops it using the work of the psychoanalytic thinkers, Austrian Sigmund Freud (1856–1939) and his French successor, Jacques Lacan, who was very influential in the 1950s and 1960s. Not only is the thetic phase the starting point for signification, it is a stage in the development of the child's subjectivity:

> In our view, the Freudian theory of the unconscious and its Lacanian development show, precisely, that thetic signification is a stage attained under certain precise conditions during the signifying process, and that it constitutes the subject without being reduced to process precisely because it is the threshold of language.
>
> (Kristeva 1984: 44–45)

These conditions are, briefly, (1) the stage Freud identified as the Oedipal stage, when, to the child's deep chagrin, it realizes that the mother is not almighty – she lacks a penis; and (2) what Lacan called the mirror stage of development, when a child at somewhere between six and eighteen months recognizes and identifies with its image in a mirror (or mirror-equivalent). The Oedipal stage raises the fear in the (male) child that it might also come to lack a penis (the fear of castration) and so it transfers its maternal attachment to its father. (Freud deemed women "the dark continent" and had little that was very convincing to say about their development. Still, we are told that, as an analog to the boy's fear of castration, girls suffer from penis envy and thus will also turn their focus onto the realm of language.) The mirror stage raises the awkward situation of needing to identify with an alien image (that is decidedly not oneself) in order to have a primordial notion of being an "I"; the child has to identify with the fictive unity it sees in the mirror and set aside the discordance of its own body that cannot even stand on its own. With these events, the child is no longer in the warm cocoon of the *chora*; it becomes dimly aware of its distinctness from its surroundings – that what surrounds it is *other* than itself. Thus, writes Kristeva:

> we view the thetic phase – the positing of the *imago*, castration, and the positing of semiotic motility – as the place of the Other, as the precondition for signification, i.e., the precondition for the positing of language. The thetic phase marks a threshold between two heterogeneous realms: the semiotic and the symbolic.
>
> (1984: 48)

Now the child is at the threshold of using language as a means of orderly communication, of beginning to be able to learn the rules of grammar and syntax, of knowing that things have names and can be named, and of begining its command of language as a system of signs. Now it is at the brink of the symbolic.

By the symbolic, Kristeva means what I have just described as "orderly communication": discourse that uses the normal rules of syntax and semantics to convey meaning. Some kind of communication is patently more symbolic than others: the language of science and logic, or the instructions that come with something you need to assemble (no one wants poetic language then!). Whenever we want to mean what we say and say what we mean, with as little ambiguity as possible, we are trying to speak symbolically. So why does Kristeva use the rather esoteric word, *symbolic*? Because even the most plain-spoken communication has a rupture within it: the rupture Ferdinand de Saussure (1857–1913), the Swiss linguist and founder of structural linguistics, saw as the gap between signifier and signified, that is, the double aspects of a term with its sound-image, on the one hand, and its meaning, on the other. To this point, Kristeva writes that the scission between semiotic and symbolic is marked by a break within the symbolic itself – between signifier and signified:

> *Symbolic* would seem an appropriate term for this always split unification that is produced by a rupture and is impossible without it. Its etymology makes it

AFFECTS AND AFFECTIVE

Most English dictionaries consider these words obsolete, but they are very alive in psychoanalytic theory. The word *affect* refers to the manifestation of the inner drives and energy that psychoanalytic theory identifies at work within the subject. These drives could be released, resulting in discharge-affects or dammed up, resulting in tension-affects. I will often use the noun *affect* to note the ways in which such drives are manifested and the adjective *affective* to note that the origins of something can be traced back to these inner states, including the drives, energy, and emotions under the surface of any human being.

> particularly pertinent. The σύμβολον is a sign of recognition: an "object" split in two and the parts separated, but, as eyelids do, σύμβολον [sign, token, or symbol] brings together the two edges of that fissure.
>
> (Kristeva 1984: 49)

Even the most plain-spoken language is an uneasy merger between a sound-image and the meaning it is supposed to denote. The sound-image cannot be completely divested of its semiotic motility, for example the affective import of a term's alliteration and rhythm.

Sometimes the semiotic aspect of a sound-image (the signifier) will lend itself to the meaning of a term (the signified) and sometimes the signifier will work against the signified. "As a result, the 'symbol' is any joining, any bringing together that is a contract – one that either follows hostilities or presupposes them – and, finally, any exchange, including an exchange of hostility" (Kristeva 1984: 49).

THE INTERPLAY OF SEMIOTIC AND SYMBOLIC

Kristeva is offering a developmental account of how the child embarks on its worldly adventures: first, in the embrace of the *chora*, where its first sounds and gestures express and discharge feelings and energy; then through certain events it comes to see itself as separate from its surroundings and thus becomes ready to use language symbolically. But, in Kristeva's view, as the child takes up the symbolic disposition it does not leave the semiotic behind. The semiotic will remain a constant companion to the symbolic in all its communications.

How can the semiotic remain part of the signifying process? The semiotic way of signifying seems to be at odds with what we usually understand to be the purpose of signification: to transmit an intended meaning from one person to another. In this sense, Kristeva says, the semiotic is "definitely heterogeneous to meaning" (1980: 133). But this does not mean that the semiotic is a stranger to meaningfulness; it is "always in sight of it or in either a negative or surplus relationship to it" (ibid.: 134):

> It goes without saying that, concerning *a signifying practice*, that is, a socially communicable discourse like poetic language, this semiotic heterogeneity posited by theory is inseparable from what I call, to distinguish it from the latter, the *symbolic* function of significance. The symbolic, as opposed to the semiotic, is this inevitable attribute of meaning, sign, and the signified object. ... Language as social practice necessarily presupposes these two dispositions [the semiotic and the symbolic], though combined in different ways to constitute *types of discourse*, types of signifying practices.
>
> (ibid.)

In the next chapter I will discuss more fully why these two types of signifying practice are inseparable, or at least why the symbolic can never be completely devoid of the semiotic. (Hint: the symbolic is always used by a speaking being.) Here I should say more about the use of this distinction in literary criticism.

GENOTEXT AND PHENOTEXT

In *Revolution in Poetic Language*, Kristeva offers a distinctive way to analyze entire literary texts. In a brief chapter entitled "Genotext and Phenotext," she uses these terms to describe two aspects of a literary text. The distinction between genotext and phenotext could be mapped onto the distinction between semiotic and symbolic – albeit roughly. The genotext is the motility between the words, the potentially disruptive meaning that is not quite a meaning below the text. The phenotext is what the syntax and semantics of the text is trying to convey, again, in "plain language." Drawing on her distinction between the semiotic and the symbolic, she shows how a text can manifest a semiotic dimension:

> Designating the genotext in a text requires pointing out the transfers of drive energy that can be detected in phonematic devices (such as the accumulation and repetition of phonemes or rhyme) and melodic devices (such as intonation or rhythm), in the way semantic and categorical fields are set out in syntactic and logical features, or in the economy of mimesis (fantasy, the deferment of denotation, narrative, etc.).

> (Kristeva 1984: 86)

Conversely, one can identify a text's phenotext by noting the "language that serves to communicate, which linguistics describes in terms of 'competence' and 'performance'" (ibid.: 87). In other words, a text operates at two levels: at the semiotic-genotext level it is a process by which the author organizes or manifests semiotic drives and energy; at the symbolic-phenotext level it is a structured and mappable piece of communication. Kristeva offers two examples to help understand the distinction. One is mathematical: genotext is to topology as phenotext is to algebra. The first points to the shape of some entity, whereas the second lays out a structure. The other example Kristeva offers is the difference between written and spoken Chinese. Written Chinese, analogous to phenotext, represents and articulates the signifying process; but only spoken Chinese, like the genotext, provides the elements necessary for an exchange of meaning between two subjects.

Nowhere is the dual aspect of texts more manifest than in the work of avant-garde writers. Analyses of these works are scattered throughout Kristeva's body of work. Here is what she has to say about one of Philippe Sollers' works:

> Now this is the point: my concern lies in the other, what is heterogeneous, my own negation erected as representation, but the consumption of which I can also decipher. This heterogeneous object is of course a body that invites me to identify with it (woman, child, androgyne?) and immediately forbids any identification; it is not me, it is a non-me in me, beside me, outside of me, where the me becomes lost. This heterogeneous objects is a body, because it is a *text*.

> (1980: 163)

Kristeva warns the reader not to be taken in by the abuse this little word, *text*, has taken. She wants the reader to see "how much risk there is in a text, how much nonidentity, nonauthenticity, impossibility, and corrosiveness it holds for those who [choose] to see themselves within it" (ibid.). Wherever there is such a disruptive genotext, the reader is put at risk, at risk of losing his or her own bounds. I will return to this thought in the next chapter.

Finally, I should mention two other terms that Kristeva coined, which made a big splash in intellectual circles, though they have not figured in much of her work since. These are *semanalysis* and *inter-textuality*. *Semanalysis* was a term she coined for the subtitle of her first book, *Semiotiké: Recherches pour une sémanalyse*. She developed this term, she later wrote, to try to "set categories and concepts ablaze," while at the same time scrutinizing the discourse of semiotic analysis (ibid.: vii). While she no longer uses the term *semanalysis*, it is certainly true that her life's work has aimed at unsettling the status quo in linguistics and semiotics. As for her term, *inter-textuality*, it is often mistakenly taken to mean the way texts intersect or can be analyzed together. But Kristeva meant something much more interesting: she meant the "*passage from one sign system to another*" – the way in which one signifying practice is transposed into another:

> The term *inter-textuality* denotes this transposition of one (or several) sign system(s) into another; but since this term has often been understood in the banal sense of "study of sources," we prefer the term *transposition* because it specifies that the passage from one signifying system to another demands a new articulation of the thetic – of enunciative and denotative positionality. If one grants that every signifying practice is a field of transpositions of various signifying systems (an inter-textuality), one then understands that its "place" of enunciation and its denoted "object" are never single, complete, and identical to themselves, but always plural, shattered, capable of being tabulated. In this way polysemy [multiple levels or kinds of meaning] can also be seen as the result of a semiotic polyvalence – an adherence to different sign systems.
>
> (Kristeva 1984: 59–60)

In other words, signifying practice is never simple and unified. It is the result of multiple origins or drives, and hence it does not produce a simple, uniform meaning. Here again, Kristeva's analysis of language demands that we attend to the field from which it is issued, and that is none other than the speaking being – what Kristeva will call *le sujet en procès* – a subject (in the other sense of the term) who is herself not a self-transparent unity.

SUMMARY

Where other linguists and philosophers have studied language as a separate, static entity, Kristeva has insisted that the study of language is inseparable from the study of the speaking being. Instead of studying language per se, she studies the signifying process, the process by which the speaking being discharges its energy and affects into its symbolic mode of signification. Her study of the signifying practice rests on psychoanalytic theory, drawing a developmental picture of the speaking being, who first begins to signify well before she learns words. First significations occur when the child is still immersed in the semiotic *chora*, the psychic space in which its early energy and drives are oriented and expressed. Even when the child matures into an adult, this semiotic dimension will continue to make itself felt.

2

THE SUBJECT IN PROCESS

The last chapter focused on Kristeva's theory of language. In discussing her views, we kept broaching a thought I have reserved for this chapter: any study of language is a study of the subject (i.e. "the subject" as an abstract person). Now we can finally attend to this idea and go further: the subject is an effect of linguistic processes. In other words, we become who we are as a result of taking part in signifying processes. There is no self-aware self prior to our use of language. At the same time, language is a signifying *process* because it is used by someone who is herself a process. Language as Kristeva studies it is inseparable from the beings that use it. And these beings, speaking beings (*parlêtres*, she calls them, combining the French words for speaking and being), are themselves constituted through a variety of different processes.

A student of Kristeva, even one who is primarily interested in her relevance to literary theory, therefore is well advised to take an excursion into Kristeva's explorations through psychoanalytic theory of how subjectivity develops. Hints of this interest can be found as early as the 1970s in *Revolution in Poetic Language*, but the bulk of her work in psychoanalytic theory occurs in the books she wrote after her return from China when, you will recall, she vowed to turn to the politics of the micro level, the level of internal experience.

As I discussed in the last chapter, Kristeva uses psychoanalytic theory to develop insights she drew from Husserl's phenomenology. She draws on both Freud and Lacan, even as she modifies their views. This is especially the case with one of the key terms of Chapter 1: the symbolic. In this second chapter, I will discuss Lacan's scheme, involving what he calls the symbolic, and then I will show how Kristeva's theory radically expands on Lacan's. We will then be in a position to understand what Kristeva calls *le sujet en procès*, translated as the subject in process/on trial.

LACAN'S INFLUENCE

In the 1950s, Jacques Lacan set himself the task of rescuing Freud's revolutionary ideas from the watered-down state to which they had been reduced by the mid-twentieth century: namely in the ego psychology prominent in America under the leadership of the Austrian psychoanalyst, Heinz Hartmann (1894–1970). According to ego psychology, the goal of psychoanalysis is to cure: to secure the ego's dominance and control over the id and the superego.

Lacan rejected this model of the ego and of psychoanalysis:

> One understands that to prop up so obviously precarious a conception certain individuals on the other side of the Atlantic should have felt the need to introduce into it some stable value, some standard of the measure of the real: this turns out to be the autonomous ego. This is the supposedly organized ensemble of the most disparate functions that lend their support to the subject's feeling of innateness.

(Lacan 1977: 230–231)

Where the ego psychologists point to an innate self, Lacan would find only an illusory unity. The ego, for him, is a tenuous and provisional construct always vulnerable to the sway of the drives. But the ego psychologists regard the ego "as autonomous because it appears to be sheltered from the conflicts of the person" (ibid.: 231). In Lacan's view, no such shelter can be had.

This may be Lacan's greatest service to Freud: recuperating the idea that the ego is an effect of largely unconscious processes, not an innate agency. For Lacan, culture, language and unconscious desires produce subjectivity.

Lacan's genius lay in his ability to bring together key insights from an array of disciplines: linguistics, anthropology, and psychoanalysis.

EGO, ID, AND SUPEREGO

In his early days, Freud noted two aspects of the self: the conscious and the unconscious. (There was also an intermediate, preconscious state.) In his later days, Freud offered a tripartite model of subjectivity in which the self is composed of, in German, "Ich," "Es," and "Über-Ich." The English equivalents are "I," "It," and "over-I" or "upper-I." For various reasons, English translators have sought to translate the perfectly plain German into obscure Latin: the Ego, the Id, and the Superego. I will follow this convention, but the reader would do well to remember the English equivalents. Freud used these three terms to designate the sense of self that one tries to develop (ego or I), the drives that often run rampant within (id or it), and the cultural censor we internalize (superego or over-I). Freud offered a useful analogy: the ego is like a driver on horseback trying to control the horse (id) while it negotiates its way through the world (superego).

Most theorists agree about what the id means: the internal biological drives, such as the drives for pleasure, self-preservation, and sometimes self-destruction. And there is little controversy about the superego: it is the internalization of society's norms – what we often call our conscience. The debate among theorists mostly revolves around what the ego is. Is it some kind of innate self, waiting to be cured or discovered? Or is it merely an effect of internal processes in relation with social forces?

For example, he noted that two of Freud's "primary processes" (fundamental inner drives) could be explained using some of the categories of literary formalism. For example, in his *Interpretation of Dreams*, Freud noted that images in dreams could work in at least two ways: one, by condensation, that is, when a symbol represents one or more things; or by displacement, when a symbol takes the place of something else. Lacan noted that what Freud identified as condensation and displacement could be explained by terms developed by the Russian formalist, Roman Jakobson (1896–1982): metaphor and metonymy. A metaphor operates by substituting one term for another, whereas a metonym operates by connecting one term to another (contiguity). A metaphor is a kind of compressed analogy, where one might, for example, call a lamb's wool its "clothing" (Lentricchia and McLaughlin 1990: 83). A metaphor makes use of the shared meaning among terms. Metonymy makes use of historical and cultural associations. Because businessmen usually wear suits, the phrase "the suits" can be metonyms for businessmen. Such analogies and connections, Lacan believes, often operate in the unconscious. Thus, we can see the effects of the unconscious in language: metaphors are evidence of condensation and metonyms are evidence of displacement. Such insights prompted Lacan to say, famously, that the unconscious is structured like a language.

Using this approach, Lacan develops much of Freud's stories, including the story of the Oedipus complex that we briefly visited in the last chapter. Recall that, in Freud's view, when the male child realizes that the mother is not almighty – that she lacks a penis – the boy turns his aspirations toward being like his father. Where Freud's concern is with the subject's father, Lacan begins to theorize "the name of the father" or "the law of the father." It is not the father per se that the child turns to but what the father represents: language and the law (including the universal taboo against incest). Where Freud addressed children's concerns (whether envy or fear, depending upon whether the subject is a girl or a boy) regarding the actual male organ, Lacan saw the concern as being about what the actual or possible lack of the organ might signify. At the biological level, the penis is the organ the boy uses for urination and later for insemination. But this use hardly begins to exhaust its meaning. At the level of the imaginary, the penis has multiple meanings. The infant imagines that the mother must have one; it comes to realize that she does not and hence he might not; it becomes a "detachable object," something he demands that his mother have. In Lacan's scheme, the penis is also what a woman demands and thus wants from a man and ultimately what she seeks by having a child. Of course, the imaginary penis is phantasmatic and leads to the function that the phallus has as the ultimate signifier. The phallus, Lacanians are quick to insist, is not the penis. It is a signifier exchanged in the symbolic realm. It does much work. For one, because it is linked, however fictively, to the penis, it signifies what women lack and what men have. In this sense, the phallus constitutes sexual difference: the symbol of women's lack and men's plenitude. But men only "have" the phallus to the extent that they have a woman around who wants what he has. Men, thus, need women to be constituted as lacking in order for them to have the illusion that they have the phallus and the power that comes with it. But since the phallus is a signifier and not an organ, no one can ever have it. No matter how much one might demand the penis as an imaginary object (for a man, in himself, for a woman, in a man), one can never have what one "really" wants: the power of the phallus, to be loved and recognized as powerful, to be complete. No object can ever satisfy this demand. One is never sated: the result of this process is desire. In Lacan's scheme, people use words in a vain attempt to get what they want, but they do not know what they really want. Lacan thus holds up the phallus as the ultimate signifier; it is the signifier of something that can never be articulated or had, yet oddly the reason why we speak at all: to try to get what we want.

Let me explain the story a bit more fully. At first the child is born into a realm of plenitude, a fullness that it feels in its mother's embrace, in having all its needs met even before they are recognized as needs. This is certainly the case in utero (at least for a healthy fetus): nourishment is constant, so there is never hunger, the lights are always dim, sounds are always muffled, and the temperature is always body temperature. (This prenatal portion of the story is my addition to Lacan's story.) This plenitude continues in its early life, until, at least, the infant realizes that there is a gap between a need and its satisfaction. The mother becomes the object of the infant's concerns. But she is not an object as distinct from himself but in connection to himself, as its first *imago*, meaning a phantasm – an object conceived to be located in internal or psychical reality, an object the subject reacts to as if it were real. At this time, the infant is in what Lacan calls the imaginary realm, the way "reality" appears to a preverbal, hence pre-linguistic, consciousness. As Alan Sheridan, one of Lacan's translators, notes, for Lacan the imaginary is what the infant took to be "the world, the register, the dimension of images, conscious or unconscious, perceived or imagined" (Lacan 1977: ix). In the imaginary, the infant does not distinguish between the truth or fiction of its images, symbols, and representations. It takes all its internal representations to be real.

The imaginary is one of three realms that Lacan postulated, the other two being the real and the symbolic. The real is what is outside of both the imaginary and the symbolic. It is always, as Lacan put it, "in its place," so parts of it cannot be taken out and inserted into language and symbolization. As Lacan's translator, Alan Sheridan, nicely puts it, in Lacan's thought the real

> became that before which the imaginary faltered, that over which the symbolic stumbles, that which is refractory, resistant. Hence the formula: "the real is the

impossible." It is in this sense that the term begins to appear regularly, as an adjective, to describe that which is lacking in the symbolic order, the ineliminable residue of all articulation, the foreclosed element, which may be approached, but never grasped: the umbilical cord of the symbolic.

(Lacan 1977: x)

While the symbolic always attempts to capture the real, it never can; for it is always only a substitute.

To explain Lacan's third term, the symbolic, let us go back to our infant, in its state of plenitude, in a most satisfying oneness with its primary caregiver, until it realizes two things: one, that there might be some boundaries to itself that separate it from others, boundaries (however fictive) that it glimpses in the mirror stage that I mentioned in the last chapter; two, that this mother is not all-powerful. As Freud argued, when the child realizes that the mother lacks a penis, he realizes the possibility of losing his own. As the father intervenes in the relationship with the mother, with his taboo against incest (too much love between mother and child could be incestuous), the child is forced to identify with his father. Maybe he cannot have his mother, but he may one day have another woman. With the loss of immediate gratification arises the experience of lack, the beginning of need. The child learns that language can be used to demand things, to get needs met: at first its cries signal that it is hungry or wet, and the mother comes running. But even as she satisfies these needs, she cannot satisfy the primordial desire: to have all needs met before they become needs. Wouldn't it be better if we could have everything we wanted without ever having to ask? Isn't "having to ask" always disappointing, no matter how quick the response? The child now experiences this insulting gap between need and satisfaction; it is in an ongoing state of desire, for desires that can never be met. But the infant, and later the adult, will keep trying; it will become schooled in the ways of language as it attempts, however futilely, to call out for what it thinks it needs. But it wants much more than it needs. And so the subject is always the subject of desire. This is why the ultimate signifier is the phallus: it is the representation of what one really wants, what Lacan cryptically call *le objet a*. It is what we are ultimately seeking and what we can never have. If the truth be known to ourselves, what we truly want is to be the object of the mother's unwavering love. But, if we had that, we would never become civilized, speaking beings. The story is a sad one, but it is the story of how human beings create civilization. We learn language and its accompanying arts as a kind of compensation for what we must all lose: being embraced by our mother's body. All our great buildings, novels, cultures are the effects of our loss of our mothers' thorough devotion.

The move I have charted above – of how the child becomes compelled to use language – is the move into the symbolic realm. Lacan's symbolic realm, which is not completely synonymous with Kristeva's symbolic, is the realm of language and symbols, structures and differences, law and order. Lacan suggested that, once a person has gotten a secure foothold in this realm of language, signs, and representations of all kinds with its accompanying laws (e.g. against incest), that the symbolic, not the imaginary realm, structures the subject. Once in the symbolic, the child is driven by desire and only has recourse to language. It will forever be frustrated by the gap between the signifier (sound-image) and the signified (the meaning or concept). Through the symbolic, the child stops being an infant (the speechless one). As John Lechte writes in his description of Lacan's theory: "In this order the individual is formed as subject" (Lechte 1997: 68). This is one way in which Lacan was a radical thinker: the symbolic realm of signs constitutes the subject, someone who can never try to understand herself separated from the way her unconscious is structured – like a language. The imaginary is territory lost to analysis. One can never ignore, Lacan writes, "the symbolic articulation that Freud discovered at the same time as the unconscious" (1977: 191).

Now we can begin to see how Kristeva parts company with Lacan. For one thing, she disagrees about the point in time at which the infant begins to differentiate itself from its mother. She places this break before the mirror stage, at an earlier time, when the infant begins to expel from itself what it finds unpalatable. This is the process she calls *abjection*, which I will discuss in detail in the next chapter.

For another, Kristeva suggests that the child begins to learn the ways of the symbolic – of culture – from its mother and not just its father. Recall from Chapter 1 Kristeva's notion of the *chora*, the psychic space in which the infant resides and in which it expresses its energy. Insofar as the mother is the child's primary caregiver, the *chora* is a maternal space. The child orients its energy in relation to its mother – who is not yet an "object" for the child "subject." There is not yet any subject–object distinction. The child experiences plenitude without

NARCISSISM

In Freud's model of ego and id, the id is understood as a wealth of energies and drives, one of which is the libido, that is, erotic or sexual feeling. "Normally" this libido will invest itself ("cathect" onto) other people. But in infancy and sometimes later it may be focused on itself. At such times, the subject is being a narcissist – someone in love with himself, just as the Greek mythological figure, Narcissus, fell in love with his own image in the water. Freud distinguished between *primary narcissism*, which is what the infant experiences in the *chora* (to use Kristeva's term) and *secondary narcissism*, which is "a withdrawal of the ego from the world of objects even after the ego has been constituted and taken love objects" (Oliver 1993: 71). Freud changed his model of narcissism over time (see ibid.), abandoning the notion that primary narcissism was a stage in favor of a model of narcissism as "an ongoing structure of the ego" (ibid.). Kristeva rejects altogether the idea of primary narcissism as a stage of development and develops Freud's later notion that it is a structure. In Kristeva's theory, the narcissistic structure provides a way for the child to start incorporating and thus mimicking what is other to itself, even before it has a concept of a self–other distinction. This narcissistic structure, which is already evident in its imaginary realm of the semiotic *chora*, paves the way for the infant to become a subject in a signifying order.

differentiation. In Lacan's terms, the child is in the imaginary realm. In Freud's terms, the child is experiencing primary narcissism.

As I have noted in the box above, Kristeva borrows and develops Freud's notion that primary narcissism is a structure. In this structure, the infant imagines that "the breast," which is really its mother's, is part of itself. As Kelly Oliver notes:

Kristeva compares the infant's incorporation of the breast to the subsequent incorporation of "the speech of the other." She explains that through incorporating the speech of the other the infant incorporates the pattern of language and thereby identifies with the other. In fact, it is the incorporation of the patterns of language through the speech of the other that enables the infant to communicate and thus commune with others. And through the ability to "assimilate, repeat, and reproduce" words, the infant becomes like the other: a subject.

(Oliver 1993: 72)

Well before the mirror stage that Lacan identified, the infant begins to experience a logic that allows it eventually to learn the ways of language and culture. Even in this "uncivilized" maternal space, the child begins to learn the language of civilization.

This brings me to the third way in which Kristeva differs from Lacan: Kristeva argues that the imaginary is not a lost territory. The psycho-analyst can find its traces. It continues to be discernible in the semiotic mode of signification. Even the real is not necessarily "always in its place," outside of signification. As she said in one interview:

> As far as Lacan's ideas go – the Real, the Imaginary, and the Symbolic – I think it extremely difficult, if not impossible, to translate one theory into another theory, because if one does, one ends in confusion and loses the specificity of each author and each approach. So I would not like to perform this reduction.
>
> (Guberman 1996: 22–23)

With this caveat, she continues:

> But it does seem to me that the semiotic – if one wants to find correspondences with Lacanian ideas – corresponds to phenomena that for Lacan are in both the real and the imaginary. For him the real is a hole, a void, but I think that in a number of experiences with which psychoanalysis is concerned – most notably, the narcissistic structure, the experience of melancholia or of cata-strophic suffering and so on – the appearance of the real is not necessarily a void. It is accompanied by a number of psychic inscriptions that are of the order of the semiotic. Thus perhaps the notion of the semiotic allows us to speak of the real without simply saying that it's an emptiness or a blank; it allows us to try to further elaborate it.
>
> (ibid.)

THE SPEAKING BEING

So it might be useful to find a correlation – albeit with caution – between Kristeva's semiotic and Lacan's imaginary, as well as between Kristeva's symbolic and Lacan's symbolic. But a major difference is that, in Kristeva's view, the pre-symbolic dimension is never out of range. The semiotic *chora*, with its affect-driven modes of signification, remains a companion in the process of signification. Kristeva shares Lacan's view that the subject is an effect of its linguistic practice, but

now we must include semiotic linguistic practice! Recall the theme of
Kristeva's major work, *Revolution in Poetic Language*: poetic language
leads to a shattering of discourse:

> Because of its specific isolation within the discursive totality of our time, this
> shattering of discourse reveals that linguistic changes constitute changes in
> the *status of the subject* – his relation to the body, to others, and to objects; it
> also reveals that normalized language is just one of the ways of articulating the
> signifying process that encompasses the body, the material referent, and
> language itself.

(Kristeva 1984: 15–16)

Moreover, in Kristeva's theory, the symbolic is not always the most
powerful mode: "On the contrary, the signifying economy of poetic
language is specific in that the semiotic is not only a constraint as is the
symbolic, but it tends to gain the upper hand at the expense of the
thetic and predicative constraints of the ego's judging consciousness"
(1980: 134). This means that the speaking being is not a stable subject.
He or she is something else altogether: a subject in process.

To explain this key idea, perhaps it is best to start with a hint offered
in *Revolution in Poetic Language*. Early in the text she suggests that a
dialectical notion of the signifying process would show how "signifiance
puts the subject in process/on trial [*en procès*]" (1984: 22).

Here is her first mention of *le sujet en procès*, translated variously as
the subject-in-process or the subject-on-trial. The French phrase *en
procès* has a double allusion to both "in process" and under legal duress.
The signifying process – which, with the semiotic, can be transgressive, disruptive, even revolutionary – puts *le sujet en procès*. How so?

SIGNIFIANCE

"Signifiance," writes Kristeva's translator, Leon Roudiez, "refers to the work
performed in language (through the heterogeneous articulation of semiotic
and symbolic dispositions) that enables a text to signify what representa-
tive and communicative speech does not say" (Kristeva 1980: 18). This is a
term Kristeva often uses to be more specific than what is connoted by *significance*, the more general meaning of a term. *Signifiance* is the meaning
produced by the semiotic in conjunction with the symbolic.

Recall Kristeva's distinction between the semiotic and the symbolic. The semiotic is the more archaic, unconsciously driven, one might say even ravenous mode of signifying. When it seeps out in signification, as it does in avant-garde poetry, it disrupts the more orderly, symbolic effort at communication. It also displays and amplifies the subject's lack of unity. In *Revolution in Poetic Language*, this disruptive aspect of signification seems limited to poetic language, but, in her later works, Kristeva extends semiosis (for Kristeva, the way the semiotic helps produce meaning, however polysemic) to other texts and signifying practices. No living, speaking being is immune from semiotic disruptions. Moreover, no speaking being could function sanely unless it expresses the semiotic in some way.

Nearly twenty years later, after more than a decade of intense work in psychoanalytic theory and practice, Kristeva develops this theme. Drawing on Lacan, Kristeva writes that the "imaginary is a kaleidoscope of ego images that build the foundation for the subject of enunciation" (1995: 104). These images primarily arise from the identifications and

PSYCHE AND SOMA

For most of the history of Western thought, philosophers have made a sharp distinction between the mind and the body, or, to use the Greek terms, between psyche and soma. The mind/body dichotomy plays into another distinction prevalent in the West – the one between culture and nature – with "culture" being the way that human beings have civilized their world with their learned ways (minds) and "nature" being the world in its raw state, the province of human beings in their animality (bodies). These terms are usually seen as diametrical opposites, hence the dualistic thinking that we have inherited, which keeps us making other dichotomies, such as active/passive, reason/passion, masculine/feminine, etc. Beginning in the nineteenth century, though, a series of philosophers (including Nietzsche, Derrida, and the French philosopher, Maurice Merleau-Ponty (1908–1961)) have tried to move beyond these dichotomies. Kristeva is part of this trajectory. Much of her work targets these distinctions, showing how bodily energies permeate our signifying practices, hence how body and mind can never be separated. In this project, she draws heavily from Freud, for whom the id, with all its libidinal energies, was not merely a biological entity. After all, the id is part of the psyche.

investments the subject makes with others – for example, early on with the mother, at one point with its image in a mirror, later with a lover or an analyst. These identifications give the subject an imaginary sense of self which allows him or her to start speaking in a coherent fashion (rather than in the babblings of an infant or madman). It is in the imaginary realm that an "I" begins to develop – thanks to its putatively *false* identifications ("I" am not one and the same as that image in the mirror).

We should note also that Kristeva is now making biological claims about the imaginary, which she ties to the "drive representatives particular to the lower layers of the brain" (ibid.). "Thus [the imaginary] can act as a relay between these layers and the cortex that controls linguistic production, thereby constituting supplementary brain circuits able to remedy any psychobiological deficiencies" (ibid.).

Kristeva put her theory to work in her own psychoanalytic practice when she was seeing a boy who had difficulty "accessing the symbolic," that is, speaking. It is not terribly uncommon for an analyst to treat a child with delayed language development. Instead of treating his problem head on, though, Kristeva focused on what she saw as the foundation of the symbolic: the imaginary realm of signification with its accompanying semiotic modes of signification. Picking up again her distinction between the semiotic and the symbolic, Kristeva writes that she distinguished

> between the *semiotic*, which consists of drive-related and affective *meaning* organized according to primary processes whose sensory aspects are often nonverbal (sound and melody, rhythm, color, odors, and so forth), on the one hand, and *linguistic signification* that is manifested in linguistic signs and their logico-syntactic organization, on the other.
>
> (1995: 104)

This linguistic (that is, symbolic) level "requires that supplementary biological and psychological conditions be met" (ibid.). In other words, the semiotic/imaginary level has to function before one could ever start speaking. So, in her treatment of the boy with delayed language, Kristeva took to singing. She and he began communicating through operas. They made up songs together, speaking in melody. The patient, Paul, took increasing pleasure in hearing his own voice. As he became more adept at communicating in song, he began to use his new oral skills in everyday speech. Kristeva's unconventional treatment focused on strengthening Paul's symbolic realm obliquely, via the semiotic mode of signification, here in the form of song. The stronger Paul's imaginary realm became, the more able he was to engage in symbolic communication.

The case of Paul shows the importance of the semiotic, imaginary field in making us into speaking beings. Without the semiotic, our language would have no force; it would be devoid of meaning. Without semiotic force, we would be like bad actors when we spoke, as if we were merely reading words off a page. Kristeva's theory of the semiotic, along with her insistence that the imaginary is an ever-present territory in our lives as speaking beings, helps her in both psychoanalytic theory and in literary criticism. If the imaginary were lost, she could not use it to help those who have lost access to the symbolic (as trauma victims often do) or to help us understand the literature handed down from so many suffering artists.

AN OPEN SYSTEM

Kristeva's theory of *le sujet en procès* gives rise to another key idea: that subjectivity occurs in an open system. Kristeva borrows this notion from biologists who, she says:

> think that a living being is not merely a structure but a structure open to its surroundings and other structures; and that interactions occur in this opening that are of the order of procreation and rejection, and that permit a living being to live, to grow, to renew itself.
>
> (Guberman 1996: 26)

One might contrast this view with the conventional understanding of subjectivity: that we are all discrete beings learning to act independently and autonomously. The Western ideal, since the eighteenth century at any rate, has been that each individual should act of his own rational accord, freed from the untoward influence of others. Against this backdrop, what Kristeva is saying seems, as she says, scandalous.

Instead of a model of the self that is stable and unified, Kristeva offers us one of a self that is always in process and hetereogeneous. The self's affective energies continue to destabilize any given self-understanding. Moreover, we are also affected by the people around us, especially the

people we love. Consider a point mentioned in the box above on narcissism: the id is comprised of energy that needs to be invested somewhere. In narcissism, it is invested in oneself. But otherwise, it is
invested in the people we love and, if we happen to be in psychoanalysis, in our analyst (this is part of the process known as
transference). These energy transfers are never made once and for all.
We will get feedback from these others, energy returned that will
shape our future actions and self-understanding:

> As implied in modern logical and biological theories dealing with so-called
> "open systems" (von Forster, Edgar Morin, Henri Atlan), *transference* is the
> Freudian self-organization, because the psychic functioning of transference is
> fundamentally dependent on the intercourse between the living-symbolic
> organism (the analysand) and the *other*. It has already been observed that this
> opening up to the other plays a decisive role in the evolution of species as well
> as in the maturing of each generation, or in every individual's particular history.
> But it can be said that with Freud, for the first time, the *love relationship*
> (imaginary as it might be) as reciprocal identification and detachment (trans-
> ference and countertransference) *has been taken as a model of optimum psychic
> functioning.*
>
> (Kristeva 1987: 14)

Whenever people are in a relationship together, there is a to and fro
of energy, desire, and memory. One person's excess may be offset by
the other's response; the two continue to respond to each other in some
way or another, keeping up a kind of oscillation. While the love relationship has its promises, it also has its dangers. A more promising
relationship for *le sujet en procès* (as such) is the relationship between
patient (analysand) and analyst. Here the subject can work through the
maladies that afflict her. Some of these will be addressed in the coming
chapters.

SUMMARY

Kristeva has made advances in the fields of semiotics, psychoanalysis, literary criticism, and moral and political theory. She has advanced the work of the French psychoanalyst and theorist, Jacques Lacan, in bringing together linguistics and psychoanalysis (as in his notion that the unconscious is structured like a language). Where Lacan argued that the "imaginary" realm is beyond the ken of analysis, that the symbolic realm is really what matters in understanding subjectivity, Kristeva argues that the imaginary realm can be discerned and should be attended to, thanks to its traces in the semiotic mode. This realm is always in play in our more poetic and evocative means of signification. In other words, the symbolic "law of the father," that is, the orderly aspects of our signifying practices, never triumphs over what she calls the semiotic (the more fluid, playful, instinctual aspects of our signifying practices). This means that signification is not a straightforward matter, that it is always disrupted by more archaic impulses. It also means that, as speaking beings, we are always works in progress. Our subjectivity is never constituted once and for all.

3

ABJECTION

In this chapter I will explain one of the most fundamental processes of the subject in process: what Kristeva calls abjection, the state of abjecting or rejecting what is other to oneself – and thereby creating borders of an always tenuous "I."

As I described it in the last chapter, the imaginary/semiotic realm is seen as a necessary precondition for symbolic, linguistic articulation. This is one side of the dialectic that Kristeva marks out between the semiotic and the symbolic. But there is also, in Kristeva's work, the negative side, where the semiotic or imaginary realm seems to threaten to disrupt the orderly symbolic realm. Again, we saw this in *Revolution in Poetic Language*. And it is a theme that continues throughout her work. It figures most prominently in her later book, *Powers of Horror*, originally published in 1980.

Powers of Horror takes the reader back to the brink of how subjectivity is constituted in the first place, that is, to how a person comes to see him- or herself as a separate being with his or her own borders between self and other. Beings do not spring forth into the world as discrete, separate subjects. According to Kristeva, our first experience is of a realm of plenitude, of a oneness with our environment, and of the semiotic *chora*. The infant comes into being without any borders. These must be developed. How these borders are developed – how the "I" forms – is one of the central concerns of psychoanalytic theory.

As I mentioned earlier, Lacan argued that subjectivity arises when an infant at some point between six and eighteen months of age catches a glimpse of himself in a mirror (or some equivalent) and takes the image to be himself. As I mentioned earlier, this identification of oneself with an image is false, because the self and the image are not one and the same. But, nonetheless, this identification helps the infant develop a sense of unity in himself. Where before experience may have been of flux, of a series of experiences and sensations, now there is an idea that the self is a unitary being, a subject separate from others.

BEFORE THE MIRROR STAGE

Kristeva agrees that the mirror stage may bring about a sense of unity, but she thinks that, even before this stage, the infant begins to separate itself from others in order to develop borders between "I" and other. The infant develops these by a process she calls abjection, a process of jettisoning what seems to be part of oneself. The abject is what one spits out, rejects, almost violently excludes from oneself: sour milk, excrement, even a mother's engulfing embrace. What is abjected is radically excluded but never banished altogether. It hovers at the periphery of one's existence, constantly challenging one's own tenuous borders of selfhood. What makes something abject and not simply repressed is that it does not entirely disappear from consciousness. It remains as both an unconscious and a conscious threat to one's own clean and proper self. The abject is what does not respect boundaries. It beseeches and pulverizes the subject.

Kristeva's examples are graphic. She speaks of curdling milk, dung, vomit, and corpses, and of how one retches at their presence. All this is to show the violence by which one jettisons phenomena that both threaten and create the self's borders:

> Food loathing is perhaps the most elementary and most archaic form of abjection. When the eyes see or the lips touch that skin on the surface of milk – harmless, thin as a sheet of cigarette paper, pitiful as a nail paring – I experience a gagging sensation and, still farther down, spasms in the stomach, the belly; and all the organs shrivel up the body, provoke tears and bile, increase heartbeat, cause forehead and hands to perspire. Along with sight-clouding dizziness, *nausea* makes me balk at that milk cream, separates me from the mother and father who proffer it. "I" want none of that element, sign of their

desire; "I" do not want to listen, "I" do not assimilate it, "I" expel it. But since the food is not an "other" for "me," who am only in their desire, I *expel* myself, I spit *myself* out, I abject *myself* within the same motion through which "I" claim to establish *myself*.

(Kristeva 1982: 3)

Another phenomenon that sets off abjection is the presence of a cadaver. Here the very border between life and death has been broken, with death seeming to "infect" the body. And we who are faced with a corpse experience the fragility of our own life. Here I am, bodily wastes and all, face-to-face with the ultimate border: "If dung signifies the other side of the border, the place where I am not and which permits me to be, the corpse, the most sickening of wastes, is a border that has encroached upon everything. It is no longer I who expel, 'I' is expelled" (ibid.: 4). The corpse is the abject reminder that I will cease to be, of "that elsewhere that I imagine beyond the present" (ibid.). The presence of a corpse violates my own borders:

Deprived of world, therefore, I *fall in a faint*. In that compelling, raw, insolent thing in the morgue's full sunlight, in that thing that no longer matches and therefore no longer signifies anything, I behold the breaking down of a world that has erased its borders: fainting away.

(ibid.)

The corpse does not represent something, as a symbol might; it is a direct "infection" of my own living: "It is death infecting life. Abject. It is something rejected from which one does not part, from which one does not protect oneself as from an object" (ibid.). The abject continuously violates one's own borders; it is sickening yet irresistible. "Imaginary uncanniness and real threat, it beckons to us and ends up engulfing us" (ibid.).

THE ABJECT MOTHER

But the most pointed case of abjection is this: the abject mother. Recall that abjection first arises when the infant is still in an imaginary union with its mother, before it has recognized its image in a mirror, well before it begins to learn language and enter Lacan's symbolic realm. The infant is not yet a subject. It is not quite yet on the borderline of subjectivity. Abjection will help it get there. And the first "thing" to be abjected is the mother's body, the child's own origin. As Kelly Oliver, a philosopher who has written extensively on Kristeva, writes: "The not-yet-subject with its not-yet, or no-longer, object maintains 'itself' as the abject. Abjection is a way of denying the primal narcissistic identification with the mother, almost" (1993: 60). In order to become a subject, the child must renounce its identification with its mother; it must draw a line between itself and her. But it is so difficult to identify *her* borders: he was once in her and now here he is outside her:

> The "subject" discovers itself as the impossible separation/identity of the maternal body. It hates that body but only because it can't be free of it. That body, the body without border, the body out of which this abject subject came, is impossible.

> (ibid.)

The child is in a double-bind: a longing for narcissistic union with its first love and a need to renounce this union in order to become a subject. It must renounce a part of itself – insofar as it is still one with the mother – in order to become a self.

Even after the child negotiates this difficult passage, the abject will continue to haunt it. Kristeva's abject differs from Freud's repressed. Freud thought that many of the subject's desires had to be denied, submerged in the unconscious, in order for subjectivity and civilization to develop. Freud addresses the continual possibility of the "return of the repressed," but, so long as it doesn't return, it is well out of sight. There is no such luck with the abject. It remains on the periphery of consciousness, a looming presence, as we've seen is the case with filth and death. So, too, with the mother. In fact, this fear of falling back into the mother's body, metaphorically at least, of losing one's own identity, is what Freud identified as the ultimate source of the feeling of uncanniness or, in German, *das Unheimliche* (literally, "the un-home-like"): "We can understand why linguistic usage has extended *das Heimliche* ['the home-like'] into its opposite, *das Unheimliche*; for this uncanny is in reality nothing new or alien, but something which is familiar and old-established in the mind" (Freud 1919: 241). What could be more "familiar" than the mother's womb? The ultimate *unheimlich* place

> is the entrance to the former *Heim* [home] of all human beings, to the place
> where each one of us lived once upon a time and in the beginning . . . when-
> ever a man dreams of a place or country and says to himself, while he is still
> dreaming: "this place is familiar to me, I've been here before," we may inter-
> pret the place as being his mother's genitals or her body.

(ibid.: 368)

Freud sets up what will become Kristeva's view: that this phenomenon conjures up a memory of the self prior to its entrance into the
symbolic realm, prior to becoming a subject proper. Freud traces this
feeling of uncanniness back to "particular phases in the evolution of
the self-regarding feeling, a regression to a time when the ego had not
yet marked itself off sharply from the external world and from other
people" (ibid.: 236). Freud argued that "the uncanny is something
which is secretly familiar, which has undergone repression and then
returned from it" (ibid.: 245). He calls this phenomenon "the return
of the repressed"; Kristeva calls it "maternal abjection." But both would
certainly agree that this state is a constant companion of consciousness,
a longing to fall back into the maternal *chora* as well as a deep anxiety
over the possibility of losing one's subjectivity.

In her description of abjection, the reader can see that this process
is not a passing stage in a person's development. It remains a companion
through the whole of one's life. As a result, cultures have set up rituals
to deal with its threat. Kristeva claims that religions have served such
purposes, setting up ways to cleanse or purify. Some religions ban
certain foods or practices, not because of anything that inheres in them,
but because they threaten the identity of the self or the social order.
As societies develop and religions wane, art takes over the function of
purification, often by conjuring up the abject things it seeks to dispel.

Let me summarize what I have said about abjection. Kristeva
describes the process by which an infant emerges from the undifferentiated union it has with its mother and surroundings. It does this by
expelling, physically and mentally, what is not part of its clean and
proper self. In this way, it begins to develop a sense of a discrete "I"
even before the mirror stage of development and before learning
language. But what the child abjects is not gone once and for all.
The abject continues to haunt the subject's consciousness, remaining
on the periphery of awareness. The subject finds the abject both repel-
lant and seductive and thus his or her borders of self are, paradoxically,

continuously threatened and maintained. They are threatened because
the abject is alluring enough to crumble the borders of self; they are
maintained because the fear of such a collapse keeps the subject vigilant.

LITERATURE AND AFFLICTION: CÉLINE'S ABJECTION

Literature, in Kristeva's view, helps the author and the reader work
through some of the maladies that afflict their souls. (I use the term *soul*
here in a non-religious way, something more akin to *psyche* or *mind*
than to spirit.) These afflictions include abjection; depression, also
known as melancholia; and various neuroses and psychoses. In psychoanalytic terms, surviving these trials involves *working through* conflicts
so that the subject is not doomed to *act them out*. Literature offers
a way to help work through what afflicts us. In addition to displaying
the symptoms of some kind of malady of the soul, literature can be
cathartic.

This is certainly true for abjection. As Kristeva says of abjection and
literature:

> By suggesting that literature is [abjection's] privileged signifier, I wish to point
> out that, far from being a minor, marginal activity in our culture, as a general
> consensus seems to have it, this kind of literature, or even literature as such,
> represents the ultimate coding of our crises, of our most intimate and most
> serious apocalypses. Hence its nocturnal power.

> (1982: 208)

In nearly all of her writings, even the most psychoanalytic ones, she
continually turns to literary texts, both as a literary critic seeking to
understand the "nocturnal power" of writing and as an analyst trying to
understand the author as a subject who is working through his or her
crises. Literature, she says, "may also involve not an ultimate resistance
to but an unveiling of the abject: an elaboration, a discharge, and a
hollowing out of abjection through the Crisis of the Word" (ibid.).

In *Powers of Horror*, after graphically describing the process of abjection, Kristeva turns to two literary examples to show how abjection
works in literature, abjection's "privileged signifier": the Bible and the
work of the twentieth-century writer known as Céline. Here I take up
the latter.

NEUROSIS, PSYCHOSIS, AND BORDERLINE STATES

Psychoanalysis began as a way to treat neurosis, which, during the nineteenth century, was seen as a disease of the nerves. Having listened to many neurotics, Freud refuted this view. Now neurosis is understood as a personality disorder. There are many kinds of neuroses and most, if not all, can be treated psychoanalytically. A neurotic person is sane and probably quite aware of his or her disorder. In classical psychoanalytic theory, psychosis is quite different. Psychotic persons are often out of touch with reality and so immersed in themselves (narcissistic) that they are not good candidates for psychoanalysis – they would not be able to displace their feelings and ideas, etc. onto their analyst (this is the crucial process known as transference). People with psychoses, including schizophrenics and severe manic-depressives, will often be treated with medication primarily. Borderline patients are those whose symptoms do not fall squarely into either neurosis or psychosis, either because their symptoms defy categorization or are not severe enough to warrant being treated as psychotic (Rycroft 1968).

Using Kristeva's terminology, we could call neurotic someone who has some kind of personality disorder, but who still has a good grasp of symbolic discourse and all the significant differences that this discourse relies on (namely, subject and object). A psychotic person would be, as classical theory agrees, someone incapable of using culture's symbolic modes, namely, because this person is in a narcissistic state and not able to negotiate the differences manifest in symbolic thinking. Whenever the symbolic structure is repudiated or collapses, reality is erased for the subject (Kristeva 1989a: 46). Moroever, when the subject severs the signifying import of semiotic affects, it becomes impossible for her to say anything meaningful. (I say this to prevent any misunderstanding that symbolic = sane and semiotic = insane. Both modes are necessary for the subject to make any sense.) Kristeva's terminology also enriches our understanding of borderline patients: these are people whose borders of self are seriously threatened, who have only a tenuous hold on the symbolic, who can barely control their semiotic affects. Kristeva's theories of the various "maladies of the soul" help explain how people get to these states.

Louis-Ferdinand Céline was the pseudonym of the writer and medical doctor, Louis-Ferdinand Destouches (1894–1961). (Destouches' grandmother's first name was Céline.) Céline, as I'll refer to him here, has been called "the strongest subterranean force in the novel today." (Quotations in this section are from the Gale database entry on Louis-Ferdinand Destouches.) He broke literary ground for a panoply of future, risqué writers, including Jean-Paul Sartre, Henry Miller, Albert Camus, Samuel Beckett, Alain Robbe-Grillet, Michel Butor, William Burroughs, Thomas Pynchon, Gunter Grass, and Joseph Heller. Most of his novels were first-person narratives of misanthropic, profane, delirious old men. One biographer, Bettina Knapp, described his scenes thus: "Huge verbal frescoes loom forth, horrendous-looking giants trample about, paraplegics, paralytics, gnomes, bloodied remnants hover over the narrations; scenes of dismemberment, insanity, murder, disease parade before the readers' eyes in all of their sublime and hideous grandeur." His first novels of the 1930s were huge hits, but his novels of the years surrounding World War II repelled many of his readers, who saw in them the marks of an author who was not just a misanthrope but an anti-semite, racist, and Nazi-collaborator. After the war, he was imprisoned in Denmark, where he had been seeking refuge for fourteen months because of his Nazi sympathies; he was released because of his ill health. Following the war, he amended some of his views. His last three autobiographical novels chronicled the collapse of Europe at the end of the war. One commentator said of this final trilogy that it was "one of the great masterpieces of western art and the greatest literary masterpiece of this era."

Despite this critical acclaim, Céline remained persona non grata. It was not until the 1960s that critics and readers returned to his works. Since then the question has been how such a brilliant writer could have written such anti-semitic books. Was he simply mistaken in holding these views, misguidedly attempting to achieve peace in Europe, or was he insane? As Anatole Broyard wrote in the *New York Times Book Review*: "the relation between [Céline's] genius as a novelist and his anti-Semitism has never been satisfactorily explained."

Perhaps not. Or perhaps Broyard has not read Julia Kristeva's account of Céline's work. Kristeva devotes the last half of *Powers of Horror* to Céline. She asks: Why are we drawn to him so vigorously? His effect, she writes, "calls upon what, within us, eludes defenses, trainings, and words, or else struggles against them" (1982: 134):

> When reading Céline we are seized at that fragile spot of our subjectivity where our collapsed defenses reveal, beneath the appearances of a fortified castle, a flayed skin; neither inside nor outside, the wounding exterior turning into an abominable interior, war bordering on putrescence, while social and family rigidity, that beautiful mask, crumbles within the beloved abomination of innocent vice. A universe of borders, seesaws, fragile and mingled identities, wanderings of the subject and its objects, fears and struggles, abjections and lyricisms. At the turning point between social and asocial, familial and delinquent, feminine and masculine, fondness and murder.
>
> (ibid.: 135)

Céline is the author of abjection. It authors him, as Kristeva shows, and he authors it for the reader. When reading Céline, our own borders of self are put on trial. We begin to lose the ability to discern between inside and outside, self and other, strange and familiar. This phenomenon pushes the reader back to a stage prior to the thetic (recall Chapter 1), prior to the ability to make judgments about objects, even to judge whether something is an object and not oneself. Reading Céline, the reader's ability to prohibit and judge, an ability brought about by the thetic stage, "becomes ambiguous, grows hollow, decays, and crumbles; it is a fleeting, derisory, and even idiotic illusion" and still one "which is yet upheld" (ibid.). Céline's works do not entirely undo meaning, as the negative side of abjection would have it; they also uphold it. His texts do not simply jettison things, they also create objects, however detested. This is part of the pathology of abjection: turning the phantasm of what is abjected into a dreaded object, an object of hate.

This is how Kristeva addresses Céline's Nazism: it cannot be explained away. Given the hallucinatory, decentering, unbearable, and disintegrating nature of his writing, which for Kristeva is an expression of himself, he needed some counterweight. Céline's narrative disintegrations were concomitant with the potential disintegration of his own identity. To keep from sinking into complete madness, he clung to the kind of feeble identity that hating Jews brought him. In this he took part in the logic of any political commitment: he had the security blanket of thinking himself part of a group – those who were not Jews.

THE ILL-LOGIC OF FASCISM

Céline's narratives may be extreme, but they are not unique. All literature, Kristeva writes, is a kind of catharsis, an attempt for the writer to throw off what is foreign and impure. The Bible, with all its rituals of purification, is an early example of this. But twentieth-century literature shows most graphically how "the narrative web is a thin film constantly threatened with bursting" (Kristeva 1982: 141). All narratives attempt to create a fictive unity, a singular meaning and identity – but insofar as such unity is an effect of abjection it will have to be tenuous and it will be a tale of suffering. Céline's writing – with its ubiquitous images of death, decay, defilement, and even birth – is replete with suffering. Kristeva comments on Céline's fascination with childbirth:

> When Céline locates the ultimate of abjection – and thus the supreme and sole interest of literature – in the birth-giving scene, he makes amply clear which fantasy is involved: something *horrible to see* at the impossible doors of the invisible – the mother's body. . . . Giving birth: the height of bloodshed and life, scorching moment of hesitation (between inside and outside, ego and other, life and death), horror and beauty, sexuality and the blunt negation of the sexual.
>
> (ibid.: 155)

Here at the "door of the feminine," at the portal of what is so other to being a subject – abjection – we get a glimpse of the economy that drives Nazism and Fascism.

In Céline's anti-semitic writings, Kristeva identifies two features that help identify this economy. The first is his "rage against the Symbolic," which Kristeva finds in Céline's scathing indictments against prominent institutions of the day, including "religious, para-religious, and moral establishments (Church, Freemasonry, School, intellectual Elite, communist Ideology, etc.); it culminates in what Céline hallucinates and knows to be their foundation and forebear – Jewish monotheism" (ibid.: 178). Kristeva is alluding here to a point she had developed in an earlier chapter. As the stories within the Bible attest, the Judeo-Christian tradition is built upon the rituals of purification. The Bible tells the story of how humankind (at least in the Judeo-Christian world) develops through abjection, through cleansing rituals, where the subject is first and always needing to be cleansed. "If abomination is the lining of my symbolic being, 'I' am therefore heterogeneous, pure and impure, and as such always potentially condemnable" (ibid.: 112). How could anyone live in such a state? By developing a scheme or law that allows for this position: I am the victim and I can purify all that defiles me. The laws of God, as laid out in the Bible, certainly lead in this direction. But nothing leads there more than the development of a language that designates and thereby separates what is clean from what is unclean, holy from profane, etc. Nothing purifies the subject more than symbolic language itself. When Céline rages against the symbolic, he is raging against the heterogeneity that gave rise to a need for such a law.

The second feature that Kristeva identifies is Céline's attempt to substitute a mystical law in the place of the symbolic law. "There is an idea that can lead nations," Céline writes. "There is a law. . . . We need an idea, a harsh doctrine, a diamond-like doctrine, one even more awesome than the others, we need it for France." Instead of interventions of the symbolic order, he wants the complete and undelayed satisfaction of all desire. He wants to revert to the stage of primary narcissism, the form of self-love present in the *chora* before the subject–object distinction arises. He looks for this satisfaction in music and dance. Céline longs, Kristeva writes, for a "*material positivity*, a full, tangible, reassuring, and happy substance" that "will be embodied in the Family, the Nation, the Race, and the Body" (ibid.: 178).

There is certainly something seductive in what Céline seeks, and Kristeva finds his logic understandable – but notes that it is deadly:

> Both the enchantment of the style and libertarian spontaneity bear within themselves their own *limit*; at the very moment that they seek to escape the oppression of the thinking, ethical, or legislative Unity [of symbolic law], they prove to be tied to the deadliest of fantasies. . . . Anti-Semitism . . . is a kind of parareligious formation; it is the sociological thrill, flush with history, that believers and nonbelievers alike seek in order to experience abjection. One may suppose, consequently, that anti-Semitism will be the more violent as the social and/or symbolic code is found wanting in the face of developing abjection. . . . Do not all attempts, in our own cultural sphere at least, at escaping from the Judeo-Christian compound by means of a unilateral call

to return to what it has repressed (rhythm, drive, the feminine, etc.), converge
on the same Célinian anti-Semitic fantasy?

(ibid.: 179–180)

The anti-Semitic fantasy, then, in Kristeva's view, is an illusion that it is possible to reject the symbolic order and return wholeheartedly to the undifferentiated semiotic *chora*, to the plenitude of that early time. No matter how untenable the symbolic order might seem, going back to this archaic state spells a complete breakdown of any kind of life. We should be wary of any communitarian "thirst for sleep and jouissance" (ibid.). This thirst can only be quenched with death.

Kristeva's theory of abjection offers a powerful way to answer the question of whether Céline was deeply mistaken or mentally unbalanced. He was both, yet neither. Of course he was mistaken in his singling out of one group of people as the source of all wrongs and of thinking that allying with Hitler would bring peace. But to say he was mistaken is an unforgivable understatement. He had the same tenuous hold on the borders of subjectivity of any paranoid, borderline, hallucinating patient. But the excuse of mental instability suggests that Céline suffered from some idiosyncratic or physiological malady – when in reality what ailed Céline was the malady of a people trying to recover a plenitude, a fullness of life, at the expense of their own, or someone else's, subjectivity. (If this is insanity, it's one that cannot shirk responsibility.) Kristeva's theory of abjection shows that Céline's malady was much more significant than either a mistake or insanity would suggest.

SUMMARY

The psychical phenomenon of abjection holds a central role in Kristeva's theory of subjectivity and in her literary criticism. As a process, expelling what is deemed "other" to "oneself," it is a means for defining the borders of subjectivity. But, as a phenomenon that never entirely recedes, abjection also haunts subjectivity, threatening to unravel what has been constructed; one's own sense of self is never settled and unshaken. To keep hold of "oneself," a subject has to remain vigilant against what may undermine its borders. Kristeva argues that much literary creation is a means of this vigilance, a kind of catharsis and purging of what is deemed other or abject. But often these literary products show a dark side of humanity, the side that finds foreigners "unclean" and wants to banish anything that is either unfamiliar or, more often, uncannily too familiar.

4

MELANCHOLIA

Imagine an infant immersed in the *chora*, still in the psychic space where there is not yet any differentiation between child and mother and surroundings, where all needs are met with no discernible delay, where there is plenitude and so no need for language. There is nothing to call for, no need to distinguish between subject and object, no need to speak. Now imagine the child losing her mother. Perhaps her mother is killed in an accident, or is hospitalized, or recedes into depression. The mother fades away before the child knows that this mother was an other. The child suffers a loss she cannot articulate. Later, she will learn language and the name "mother," but she loses her mother before she has this ability to name. She suffers before she can speak. She may well recover and have a normal childhood, but then, later in life, perhaps in her early twenties as a result of some trauma, she may sink deep into depression, a depression that far exceeds the immediate trouble that precipitated it. She is listless; she moves slowly; she sleeps most of the day; she barely speaks.

LOST OBJECT OR THING?

Psychoanalytic theorists might argue among themselves about her illness – about its exact cause, about the best treatment, etc. – but they will agree about one thing: she is in mourning. Freud and later psychoanalytic theorists agree that depression, or melancholia as it used to be called, is a mourning for something lost. According to the prevailing model of depression developed by the pioneering psycho-analyst, Melanie Klein (1882–1960), the lost object is not an actual person but an "internal object." The subject feels both love and hate toward this object, love because he cannot do without it and hate be-cause he has been undermined by its loss. The subject reproaches himself. He may consider suicide as a way of killing the hated object within. If he were to go into psychoanalysis, he might learn the true target of his hostility; he may learn that he internalized the loss of some-thing outside of himself. In the classical account, depression is a mourning for a lost internal object, a mourning characterized by ambivalence and hostility.

But would this diagnosis be fitting for the young woman in the story I just told? Not according to Kristeva. The classical story accounts for depression that results from a loss suffered *after* one has made the thetic break into the symbolic (after one begins to differentiate subject from object and to speak). It does not account for the suffering of those who have lost their primary love while still in the *chora*. In these cases:

> Far from being a hidden attack on an other who is thought to be hostile be-cause he is frustrating, sadness would point to a primitive self – wounded, incomplete, empty. Persons thus affected do not consider themselves wronged but afflicted with a fundamental flaw, a congenital deficiency. Their sorrow doesn't conceal the guilt or the sin felt because of having secretly plotted revenge on the ambivalent object. Their sadness would be rather the most archaic expression of an unsymbolizable, unnameable narcissistic wound, so precocious that no outside agent (subject or agent) can be used as referent. For such narcissistic depressed persons, sadness is really the sole object; more precisely it is a substitute object they become attached to, an object they tame and cherish for lack of another. In such a case, suicide is not a disguised act of war but a merging with sadness and, beyond it, with that impossible love, never reached, always elsewhere, such as the promises of nothingness, of death.

(Kristeva 1989a: 12–13)

As opposed to the first kind of depression I described, which Kristeva calls *objectal depression*, Kristeva calls this second kind *narciss-istic depression*. Instead of feeling hostility to some internal object, the depressed narcissist feels flawed, incomplete, and wounded. This is understandable. Of course she would feel personally wounded – the loss she suffered was of part of herself, insofar as the wound was suffered before she could distinguish her mother from herself. The wound manifested itself linguistically, disrupting her ability to symbolize and to name. This is one of the primary symptoms of depression that Kristeva zeroes in on: the loss of interest, even inability, in speaking. Melancholia is a noncommunicable grief; the melancholic is wrapped up in her sadness; it is hers alone, something she cannot share in the social/symbolic realm. Of course, this is precisely the malady: a wound occurring when one is still in infancy, in the midst of what Freud called primary processes.

In Freudian theory, the term *primary* refers to the first stage of development and to what occurs unconsciously. *Secondary* is an adjective used to describe what happens post-Oedipally and consciously. Primary processes include condensation and displacement, which were briefly discussed in Chapter 2: the ways in which dream images and symbols connect. Secondary processes follow the laws of grammar and logic (Rycroft 1968: 138). When there is a loss occurring at the primary level – in the *chora*, well before the symbolic forms – the result can be narcissistic depression.

If Kristeva is right, narcissistic depression points to the importance the mother and the imaginary realm play in the child's acquisition of language. A loss suffered in the semiotic *chora* hampers one's entry into the symbolic. With the process of abjection derailed – primary love is lost before it can be expelled – the child can never properly make the break between subject and object. Lacking the ability to discern and judge – because the child has not entered the thetic phase – the child cannot name what she has lost. It will never be an *object* for her, but an unnameable *thing*. This is why the first model of depression, objectal depression, does not apply to our hypothetical example. This is why the melancholic feels wounded rather than hostile.

There is nothing to be hostile toward. All there is is a loss. "The depressed narcissist mourns not an Object but the Thing (*Chose*)," Kristeva says somewhat cryptically. This Thing is an enigmatic, indeterminate something, a "light without representation." "Let me posit the 'Thing' as the real that does not lend itself to signification, the center of attraction and repulsion, seat of the sexuality from which the

MELANCHOLIA AND DEPRESSION

In the book she wrote in 1987, *Soleil noir* or *Black Sun*, Kristeva uses the now obsolete term *melancholia* to refer to narcissistic depression, which she suggests is closer to psychosis than neurosis. (But to the extent that the melancholic has any hold on the symbolic – and most melancholics do, even if they refuse to use it – he or she is not psychotic. See Kristeva 1989a: 47.) This would mean that a melancholic is not the best candidate for psycho-analysis (see the definitions for psychosis and neurosis at the beginning of this chapter). Objectal depression could be understood as a neurosis, because the loss occurs, in Klein's view, after the child has weaned and, thus, probably post-Oedipally, after the child has learned language and of course the subject–object distinction. Such depression would be a better candidate for psychoanalysis. Still, the standard treatment for all forms of depression today is medical, whether by antidepressant medication or minerals such as lithium. Kristeva asks whether literary production might be an alternative "treatment" for depression, depression of both forms. Because both forms of depression impair the subject's willingness and ability to speak, and because Kristeva is focusing on a signifying practice as a "counterdepressant," Kristeva doesn't worry too much about the tech-nical differences between different forms of depression. She uses the terms *melancholia* and *depression* almost interchangeably.

object of desire will become separated" (Kristeva 1989a: 13). Here Kristeva is drawing on the Lacanian notion of the real, which, as I discussed in Chapter 2, is one of the three realms that Lacan posited: the real, the imaginary, and the symbolic. The real is impossible to describe, but also the ineliminable residue that resists articulation. It is there, but it is ineffable. The depressed narcissist feels this real, this Thing, bearing down upon her. "Of this Nerval [the poet Gérard de Nerval (1808–1855)] provides a dazzling metaphor that suggests an insistence without presence, a light without representation: the Thing is an imagined sun, bright and black at the same time" (ibid.). She quotes Nerval directly: "It is a well-known fact that one never sees the sun in a dream, although one is often aware of some far brighter light" (ibid.). Drawing on Nerval, she titles her book on depression and melancholia, *Soleil noir* or, in English, *Black Sun*.

SEVERED FROM THE SYMBOLIC

"Knowingly disinherited of the Thing, the depressed person wanders in pursuit of continuously disappointing adventures and loves; or else retreats, disconsolate and aphasic, alone with the unnamed Thing" (Kristeva 1989a: 13). The depressed narcissist "has the impression of having been deprived of an unnameable, supreme good, of something unrepresentable," something that "no word could signify" (ibid.). This is why the melancholic barely speaks. She sees no point. Whereas all people must eventually lose their mothers (we are all weaned, after all!), most will compensate for this lost object of desire by using language, words, to chase what has been lost, much as Lacan postulated in his story of how desire motivates one's immersion in the symbolic. But the melancholic has no such object of desire. "Consequently, for such a person, no erotic object could replace the irreplaceable perception of a place or preobject confining the libido or severing the bonds of desire," Kristeva writes (ibid.). Lacking an interest in any objects, the melancholic lacks motivation to engage in the symbolic realm – that is, to speak or write. Words seem pointless, for they are not connected to the subject's affects, desires – in short, to the semiotic *chora*. The depressed person is like an orphan in the symbolic realm.

Having turned away from symbolic, signifying practice, the melancholic makes do without the self-unity that the symbolic offers. Here we should remind ourselves of one of the functions of the symbolic, as both Lacan and Kristeva understand it: the realm of signs gives the subject a sense, however fictive, of being an "I." According to Lacan, the infant first gets this sense of unity when it recognizes its image in a mirror and takes the image to be itself. In place of the imaginary's flux and heterogeneity (where the subject experiences a disparate array of affects, images, and energy that it cannot distinguish or integrate), the realm of signs gives the infant the sense that it is an "I" – a unified, discrete being that is separate from other discrete beings. The symbolic's subject–object distinction allows for a sense of coherence, distinctness, and self-unity. Without the symbolic, the subject regresses, falling back into a realm where nothing is differentiated, so the self cannot separate itself from its heterogeneous surroundings. As a regression to an archaic state, Kristeva notes that this phenomenon is akin to what Freud called the death drive (sometimes using the Greek word for death, *thanatos*). Drawing on Freud, Kristeva says that the

THE DEATH DRIVE

In the 1910s and 1920s, Freud postulated the idea that, in addition to an instinct for pleasure and life, the subject has an instinct for death. The death drive has two parts: one directed outward as a purely destructive discharge of energy and the other directed inward as a disintegration of the living self, a wish to return to an inorganic state and homeostasis. The first of these involves a wish to kill others and the second a wish to annihilate oneself (Kristeva 1989a: 16; Rycroft 1968: 13). Usually a reference to the death drive is a reference to the self-destructive instinct.

death drive appears as a "biological and logical inability to transmit psychic energies and inscriptions," therefore destroying "movements and bonds" (ibid.: 17).

In regressing from the symbolic, the subject returns to a narcissistic state. The narcissistic structure seems to share features of the death drive. Both lead to a kind of disintegration, a threat of the loss of subjectivity. The subject loses cohesion, the ability to integrate its experiences, and it risks further disintegration. Kristeva quotes Melanie Klein:

> The early ego largely lacks cohesion, and a tendency towards integration alternates with a tendency towards disintegration, a falling into bits . . . the anxiety of being destroyed from within remains active. It seems to me in keeping with the lack of cohesiveness that under the pressure of this threat the ego tends to fall into pieces.
>
> (1989a: 19)

Kristeva builds upon Klein's view, saying that melancholics also experience this disintegration of bonds, a splitting or parceling of the self.

A UNITY OF SADNESS

But the melancholic does not simply give in to this self-destruction. She attempts to protect herself with a shield of sadness:

> Following upon the deflection of the death drive, the *depressive affect* can be interpreted as a defense against parceling. Indeed, sadness reconstitutes an

affective cohesion of the self, which restores its unity within the framework of the affect. The depressive mood constitutes itself as a narcissistic support, negative to be sure, but nevertheless presenting the self with an integrity, nonverbal though it might be. Because of that, the depressive affect makes up for symbolic invalidation and interruption (the depressive's "that's meaningless") and at the same time protects it against proceeding to the suicidal act. That protection, however, is a flimsy one. The depressive denial that destroys the meaning of the symbolic also destroys the act's meaning and leads the subject to commit suicide without anguish of disintegration, as a reuniting with archaic nonintegration, as lethal as it is jubilatory, "oceanic."

(Kristeva 1989a: 19)

Sadness gives the depressive a unity, but it is not enough to protect against the death drive that is already at work in the narcissistic structure. To the extent that she has repudiated the realm of signs, the melancholic also repudiates the sign she wears around her neck, her affect of sadness. No sign has any meaning for her and so she has little defense against the death drive.

Kristeva calls sadness "the fundamental mood of depression" (ibid.: 21). It is a kind of sign or representation – not a verbal one, but one inscribed by one's whole demeanor. As is the case with all moods or affects (including anguish, fear, and joy), sadness signals to any observer that some kind of energy displacement, stimulation, conflict or transfer has occurred within the subject. Mood "is a 'generalized transference' that stamps the *entire* behavior and all the sign systems (from motor functions to speech production and idealization) without either identifying with them or disorganizing them" (ibid.). Someone's overall affect indicates a mood, which itself indicates semiotic processes at work within the subject:

Let us say that representations germane to affects, notably sadness, are *fluctuating* energy cathexes: insufficiently stabilized to coalesce as verbal or other signs, acted upon by primary processes of displacement and condensation, dependent just the same on the agency of the ego, they record through its intermediary the threats, orders, and injunctions of the superego. Thus moods are *inscriptions*, energy disruptions, and not simply raw energies. They lead us toward a modality of signifiance that, on the threshold of bioenergetic stability, insures the preconditions for (or manifests the disintegration of) the imaginary and the symbolic.

(ibid.: 22)

Mood is an archaic form of signifiance, which, as Chapter 2 discussed, is the work performed through the semiotic as well as the symbolic dispositions, the meaning produced that could not be produced by the symbolic alone. We react to our traumas with a variety of moods. "On the frontier between animality and symbol formation, moods – and particularly sadness – are the ultimate reactions to our traumas, they are our basic homeostatic recourses" (ibid.). Some people show their frailty in the extent to which they are always drowned in their sorrows. Others show their creativity and indomitableness in a "diversification of moods, variety in sadness, refinement in sorrow or mourning" (ibid.). These creative melancholics are the ones who take part in "that adventure of the body and signs that bears witness to the affect – to sadness as imprint of separation and beginning of the symbol's sway" (ibid.); these are the novelists, poets, and artists, who have been moved to create by the black sun of melancholia.

JOURNEYING INTO THE REALM OF SIGNS

Why would a melancholic, no matter how creative, take part in an adventure of signs when, according to Kristeva, being melancholic means *repudiating* the realm of signs? Is not the melancholic – the depressed narcissist – so wrapped up in her own sadness that she does not find any point in using signs? Is not the problem of melancholia the unwillingness to substitute signs for the lost Thing? Kristeva needs a way to explain how the depressed artist would reach the realm of signs. She does this by using more of Freud's theory. She says that someone might be able to reconcile the loss of the Thing through "primary identification" with the "father in individual prehistory" (Kristeva 1989a: 13). As the scholar John Lechte explains:

The father in individual prehistory emerges prior to the formation of an object which will accompany the emergence of the subject in language; it is thus prior to any ideal, but is nonetheless the *basis* of all idealization – especially in love. The father of individual prehistory which Kristeva also calls the Imaginary Father is the basis for the formation of a successful narcissistic structure – one that enables the symbolization of loss, and the formation of desire.

(1990: 30)

Recall that, in my definition of narcissism in Chapter 2, I explained that, for Kristeva, the narcissistic structure allows the child – pre-symbolically – to start incorporating and mimicking what is other to itself, thus paving the way for the infant to become a subject in a signifying order. In the imaginary realm, while the child is beginning to lose or "negate" its mother, it also begins to incorporate or identify with an imaginary father, a phantasm of the logic of identifying one thing with another. If the structure works successfully, the child will complete its separation from its mother while at the same time learning to use words to name what he has lost – which will allow him to call out to her when he needs her. If this process is not successful, the child will be caught in limbo between loss and identification. "Ovid's Narcissus before his pool is precisely not an example of the narcissistic psychic structure" that Lechte and Kristeva are describing, "for the youth beside the pool is frozen" before he can desire an object outside himself and confirm his subjectivity. "Narcissus' death is the sign of the failure of psychic space to form due to the failure of a sense of loss to form" (ibid.).

Thus we can see more clearly what the melancholic needs to do in order to triumph over his sadness. He needs to complete his separation from the enigmatic Thing and begin to identify with the image of the logic of identification, the Imaginary Father. "Primary identification initiates a compensation for the Thing and at the same time secures the subject to another dimension, that of imaginary adherence, reminding one of the bond of faith, which is just what disintegrates in the depressed person" (Kristeva 1989a: 13–14). Identifying with this image of the logic of identification gives the subject some *faith* that one thing could possibly stand in for another, that the sound-image *mother* could connect in any fashion with the signified meaning of *mother*. It gives the subject reason to believe that there will be any comfort in the realm of signs.

NERVAL, THE DISINHERITED POET

Kristeva devotes a chapter of *Black Sun* to the poet I mentioned earlier, Gérard de Nerval (the pen name of Gérard Labrunie), whose poem "El Desdichado" ("The Disinherited") contains the phrase *soleil noir* or *black sun* – specifically, "the Black Sun of Melancholia." He certainly fits the description of a melancholic. He was born in 1808 to a brooding and humorless father, who was just completing his studies to be a medical doctor, and a mother with such a delicate physical constitution that the newborn was sent to a village near Mortefontaine to be nursed by other family members. (Most of the information for this biographical sketch is drawn from the Gale Group Database: Dictionary of Literary Biography.) Within six months his mother died of influenza. Though he never knew her, he was fascinated by her throughout his life, speaking of her often and imagining what she must have been like. His father spent the early years of the boy's life serving as a doctor for Napoleon's army and, after the son and father were reunited, their relationship was turbulent. The boy, who would become one of the innovative poets of the mid-nineteenth century, was never a particularly good student, but, by the age of sixteen, he was writing poems in his notebook. Soon he was devoting all his time to writing and traveling, helping found a literary journal with a fair-sized inheritance, and doing a little bit of diplomatic work in between. In 1832 he became entranced by the actress, Jenny Colon, whom he seems to have worshiped from afar, as he did most of the women he admired.

The major turning point in his life was in February 1841, when he suffered his first mental breakdown. As Nerval scholar, Peter Edwards writes:

> He was taken to a clinic on the rue de Picpus in the Latin Quarter and remained there for a month. Some of the letters he wrote during this internment are clearly delusional, and in reading them one begins to get a glimpse of the highly personal and intense processes of synthesis that were taking place in the poet's mind. Persons, places, and literary memories all coalesce into a labyrinth of referential confusion.

(Edwards 1999)

Five days after being released from this clinic, he landed in another, where he remained until November of that year. During this period of asylum he seems to have adopted the difficult poetic form of the sonnet, which he used exclusively for all but one or two poems for the rest of his life. Peter Edwards comments on six sonnets Nerval wrote at this time, saying,

> [they] are fascinating texts that seem to defy coherent interpretation, even as they exercise rhythmically hypnotic power on the reader. Nerval weaves into

> these sonnets of an admirable purity of form allusions to Greek and Egyptian mythology, Judaic history and theology, Christian history and theology, modern French and oriental history, personal history, and references to several literary texts. Although never published, these sonnets are seminal for Nerval [turning up in modified form in the great poems of his last years].
>
> (1999)

During the next twelve years he wrote and published extensively, working on plays, travel essays, sonnets, a comic opera, a novella, translations of German poetry, and historical essays. There is some evidence that he may have suffered two more mental crises during this period. In February 1853, he suffered another, more serious, mental breakdown from which he never completely recovered. For the last two years of his life, brief periods of lucidity and feverish work were interspersed with more psychotic breaks. On the night of 14 January 1855, he hung himself in an alley in Paris.

Clearly, from his early loss of his mother to his suicide, Nerval bears the marks of a melancholic. But also, just as clearly, he reached out to the realm of signs, putting his mood to work in the symbolic realm. Kristeva analyzes the case of Nerval through a close reading of one of his later works, the sonnet "El Desdichado" ("The Disinherited").

El Desdichado (*The Disinherited*)

1   Je suis le ténebreux, – le veuf, – l'inconsolé,
2   Le prince d'Aquitaine à la tour abolie;
3   Ma seule *étoile* est morte, – et mon luth constellé
4   Porte le *Soleil noir* de la *Mélancolie*.

5   Dans la nuit du tombeau, toi qui m'a console,
6   Rends-moi le Pausilippe et la mer d'Italie,
7   La *fleur* qui plaisait tant à mon cœur désolé,
8   Et la treille où le pampre à la rose s'allie.

9   Suis-je Amour ou Phébus? . . . Lusignan ou Byron?
10   Mon front est rouge encor du baiser de la reine;
11   J'ai rêvé dans la grotte où nage la sirène . . .

12   Et j'ai deux fois vainqueur traversé l'Achéron:
13   Modulant tour à tour sur la lyre d'Orphée
14   Les soupirs de la sainte et les cris de la fée.

1   *I am saturnine — bereft — disconsolate,*
2   *The Prince of Aquitaine whose tower has crumbled;*
3   *My only star is dead — and my star-studded lute*
4   *Bears the Black Sun of Melancholia.*

5   *In my dark night of the grave, you who brought me solace,*
6   *Give me back Posilipo and the Italian sea,*
7   *The flower that my distressed heart found so pleasing,*
8   *And the arbor where grapevine and rose grow as one.*

9   *Am I Eros or Phebus? . . . Lusignan or Byron?*
10 *My brow is still red from the queen's kiss;*
11 *I have dreamt in the cave where the siren swims . . .*

12 *And twice, I have crossed the Acheron victorious;*
13 *Modulating by turns on Orpheus' lyre*
14 *The sighs of the saint and the screams of the fay.*

(as published in *Les chimères*, 1973,
translation author's own)

Kristeva reads the poem as the disinherited melancholic's attempt to reach the realm of signs, to give a name to the Thing that he mourns. In her reading of this poem, Kristeva does three things. First, she makes it plain that the disinherited one, the narrator and, for that matter, the poet, is a melancholic. To show that the narrator fits the description of the melancholic or depressed narcissist, Kristeva addresses the title of the poem. From what is the narrator disinherited? His "only star" of line three is dead, he says, but what is this that has gone, Kristeva asks. Not an object, she answers, but the Thing. What does he have left? Here we get the brilliant and dark metaphor. Kristeva writes:

> As a result of the absorption of the "dead star" into the "lute," the "Black Sun" of "Melancholia" emerges. Beyond its alchemical scope, the "Black Sun" metaphor fully sums up the blinding force of the despondent mood — an excruciating, lucid affect asserts the inevitability of death, which is the death of the loved one and of the self that identifies with the former (the poet is "bereft" of the "star").

(1989a: 151)

Kristeva sees in Nerval's metaphor a poet deeply introspective, one who, by trying to name the sun in this way, is at the "threshold of a crucial experience." The poet is classically borderline, "on the divide between appearance and disappearance, abolishment and song, non-meaning and signs." His is a "psyche struggling against dark asymbolism" (ibid.). Kristeva would certainly categorize Nerval as someone suffering from narcissistic depression – melancholia – and not mere objectal depression.

Next, Kristeva shows how the melancholic poet attempts to master his sadness by reaching the realm of signs. But he will not write symbolically the way a "normal" writer would. He rarely if ever writes in a straight narrative form. "Narrative continuity, which beyond the certainty of syntax, builds space and time and reveals the mastery of an existential judgment over hazards and conflicts, is far from being Nerval's favorite realm," Kristeva writes. "Any narrative already assumes that there is an identity stabilized by a completed Oedipus and that, having accepted the loss of the Thing, it can concatenate its adventures through failures and conquests of the 'objects' of desire" (ibid.: 161). This kind of storytelling seems too secondary, schematic and superficial to capture Nerval's black sun.

Will the traces of that lost Thing sweep the poet away or will he carry them away? The poet's task is to find a way to name the Thing when he has no facility for naming, when the Thing is unnameable. He must somehow turn this lost enigma into an object of desire, move it from the imaginary to the symbolic. In the imaginary realm where the depressed narcissist takes refuge, there is no distinction between self and other and thus no object of sexual desire. Sexual desire for another person is something that occurs only after the subject has differentiated himself and begun to use words to name. The poet who never knew his mother, who would never approach a woman he admired from a distance, turned away from sexual desire. The women that appear in lines 10 and 11 show the narrator moving from a dominating queen to a cool siren, from a strong, threatening woman to a uterine, imaginary refuge. "We thus find only a simple, slight allusion to sexual desire and its ambivalence," writes Kristeva. "The erotic connection does, in fact, bring to their climax the conflicts of a subject who experiences both sexuality and the discourse that refers to it as destructive. One understands why the melancholy withdrawal is a fugue in the face of the dangers of eroticism" (ibid.: 158). Withdraw he might, but by doing so, by "blocking the way toward the other," it seems that the subject "sentence[s] itself to lie in the Thing's grave" (ibid.: 159).

Nerval does not lie there. Though he may lack any facility with or desire to use straight narrative, he has at his disposal the great trope of poets: metaphor. Metaphor, the substitution of one term for another, a carrying away that is never of the same order as the original, provides the poet a way to sublimate potentially destructive energy. (In psychoanalytic theory, sublimation is the process by which instincts, energy, and drives are discharged or transformed into other, usually more socially acceptable, forms.)

The melancholic poet can turn his sorrow into a sonnet:

> By means of a leap into the orphic world of artifice (of sublimation), the saturnine poet, out of the traumatic experience and object of mourning, remembers only a gloomy or passional tone. He thus comes close, through the very components of language, to the lost Thing. His discourse identifies with it, absorbs it, modifies it, transforms it: he takes Eurydice out of the melancholy hell and gives her back a new existence in his text/song.
>
> (ibid.: 160)

Does Nerval successfully reach the realm of signs? Kristeva notes that the references throughout Nerval's poem are uprooted, transposed, inserted in a poetic web, multivalent, and undecidable. Often his language serves more as a gesture pointing to the lost Thing, rather than as signs of some signified object. Like the other signs in the poem, the star is a sign without a signified, it signals without having a referent. The same is true of many other nouns in the poem; they often serve more as concatenations than as designations of some object.

But it matters little whether the reader knows, for example, who Phebus or Lusignan or Byron are. The constellation of names creates the poet's own symbolic family. "The litaneutical, hallucinatory gathering of their names allows one to suppose," writes Kristeva, "that they might merely have the value of signs, broken up and impossible to unify, of the lost Thing" (ibid.: 157).

Given that the poet committed suicide a year after publishing this final version of the poem, we already know the ultimate answer to the question of whether Nerval succeeded. But, Kristeva finds, his writing did provide him with temporary salvation: "It can thus be understood that the triumph over melancholia resides as much in founding a symbolic family (ancestor, mythical figure, esoteric community) as in constructing an independent symbolic object − a sonnet," she writes.

"Attributable to the author, the construction becomes a substitute for the lost ideal in the same way as it transforms the woeful darkness into a lyrical song that assimilates 'the sighs of the saint and the screams of the fay'" (ibid.: 162).

If Nerval succeeded in overcoming his depression, it was only temporary. He did in the end commit suicide. But can any of us ever be sure of complete success in shoring up our subjectivity? No, Kristeva's work suggests: "Even the soundest among us know just the same that a firm identity remains a fiction" (ibid.: 257). To the extent that anyone is a subject in process and on trial, literary creation, the sublimation of death-dealing desire into art, is a life-enhancing venture.

SUMMARY

Melancholia and depression are conditions in which the speaking being loses or turns away from the realm of signs. By being brought back to a narcissistic realm of images and lost Things rather than a realm of objects and signs, the depressed person has a double challenge: to complete the process of losing objects that it might desire, so that it can begin the process of substitution and identification. Literary creation offers a way for the melancholic to proceed, to try to turn his or her sadness and sorrow into a symbolic object, to share again in the community of other speaking beings.

5

HERETHICS

For someone commonly known in the English-speaking world as one of the major three "French feminists" (along with Hélène Cixous and Luce Irigaray), Julia Kristeva has had surprisingly little to say about feminism. Sometimes what she has to say is quite derogatory, calling some kinds of feminism "the last of the power-seeking ideologies" (Kristeva 1982: 208). Kelly Oliver explains the discrepancy as follows:

> When American theorists and practitioners talk about feminism they refer to a multifaceted conglomerate of different views and strategies that cannot be easily reduced to a single element. When French theorists and practitioners talk about feminism, however, they are referring to a specific political movement in France. So when "The French Feminists" refuse to be identified as feminists this does not mean that they would not identify with some of the goals and strategies of feminism in the American [and we could add English] context. What they are rejecting is a specific movement in France that many of them think engages in, and merely replicates, oppressive bourgeois logics and strategies of gaining power.
>
> (Oliver 1993: 164)

So, though Kristeva may have a tendentious relationship with some of the feminist movement, we need not interpret this as a sign of antipathy to the goals of feminism in general. Close attention to her writing on feminism shows that, though Kristeva has a complicated relationship to feminist thought, she is in fact concerned with bettering women's situation. She would like to find a way to remove women from the straitjacket of old, sexist thinking that marginalizes women from the currents of social, symbolic thought. But she also wants to avoid the temptation to say that women can be "just like" men. As this chapter will discuss, Kristeva is looking for a "third way" for feminism to proceed, a way for women to feel free to have children *and* create culture, to be of the body and the mind. She resists any temptation to see these two poles – culture and nature – as antithetical and mutually exclusive. In her thought, the reader can find a way to bring together the biological and the cultural world we inhabit.

In so doing, Kristeva develops a new conception of ethics. Traditionally, for all the divergence of views within moral philosophy, ethical thought in the West has been nearly unanimous in conceiving of ethical agents as discrete individuals. Drawing on Freud and Lacan, as well as her own experience of pregnancy and motherhood, Kristeva challenges the dominant view that self and other can be clearly demarcated. She finds in the experience of pregnancy a relation to an "other" who is never wholly other but at the same time not entirely oneself. The love that a soon-to-be mother feels for this not-quite-other being provides Kristeva with a new model of ethical relationship.

This chapter, along with the following one, provides an overview and an assessment of Kristeva's writing on feminism, maternity, and the ethics she derives from her view of the maternal relation.

KRISTEVA'S CRITICS

To a large degree, feminist theory in England and America has addressed the political, cultural, and sociological practices and institutions that marginalize or oppress women. Feminist philosophers in France tend to take a different approach, focusing on what we might call the *metaphysical* suppositions that underlie sexist institutions and practices. As a branch of philosophy, metaphysics is the study of reality above or beyond physics, that is, beyond scientific or factual questions about the world. Where many feminists will look at the empirical facts that bind women, Kristeva and others like her will look at the deeper questions. One of these questions is the question of sexual difference. Many of the French feminists, Kristeva included, take seriously the proposition that there is some fundamental difference between the sexes – not just a difference that could be identified biologically or psychologically, but a difference in how men and women are constituted as such, a difference, for example, in the way that the symbolic realm with its inherent logical structures (recall the discussion of Saussure in earlier chapters) of identity and difference positions women as different from or merely the negative of men. Is there "woman" as such – or is she merely the play of signs in the symbolic realm? That is the kind of question Kristeva takes up when she takes up feminist theory. And that is the very kind of question that makes many feminists in England and America very nervous. Any inquiry into whether or not there is an "essence" of "woman" conjures up images of old sexist classifications of woman as possibly inferior to men.

Accordingly, a familiar criticism leveled by feminist critics against Julia Kristeva's philosophy is that it is essentialist. The term *essentialism* has been used in many different ways – often as an accusation: (1) as a practice of making false generalizations; (2) as offering a biological explanation for a psychological trait; and (3) as providing a substantive account of what it is to *be* a certain kind of thing. Feminists are often accused of the first kind of essentialism, but the "French feminists" seem to be accused of the second and third sort. During the 1980s and 1990s, leading feminist critics in the English-speaking world, such as Nancy Fraser, Judith Butler, Elizabeth Grosz, and Toril Moi, mounted these kinds of charges against Kristeva. They took issue with her conceptions of the *chora*, maternity, and the semiotic, arguing that, in invoking these, Kristeva is positing some female essence. Critics linked her idea of the *chora* with a maternal receptacle, which they linked with her semiotic aspect of signification and with woman. They made claims about Kristeva's supposed "compulsory maternity," about her quietude in the face of an "implacable symbolic structure." The concern among many feminists has been that, in Kristeva's philosophy, woman is linked necessarily with the maternal and that she is powerless to change a male-driven symbolic order.

"Ahistorical, biologically reductive, . . . universalist – the list of crimes of which Kristeva is found guilty, under the guise of essentialism, abounds," notes the feminist philosopher, Tina Chanter (Chanter 1993: 182). The charges revolve around two points. One is that Kristeva works within a psychoanalytic model, which many critics take to be patent proof that she accepts the sex roles that psychoanalytic

theory recognizes. Accordingly, the philosopher, Chris Weedon, crit-
icizes Kristeva on the grounds that "to take on the Freudian and
Lacanian models is implicitly to accept the Freudian principles of
psycho-sexual development with their universalist patriarchal implications and their reduction of subjectivity to sexuality" (as quoted in
Chanter 1993: 192, note 7). This charge makes three questionable
assumptions: (1) that to use psychoanalytic theory is to accept it in toto;
(2) that psychoanalytic theory necessarily relies on universal rather than
culturally specific sex roles; and (3) that it recognizes only sexual or
biological influences. The other charge often leveled against her is that,
in her own linguistic theory, the semiotic (poetic, disruptive, potentially revolutionary) aspect of communication supposedly draws on
or is identified with the maternal body and that this semiotic aspect
is ultimately powerless in the face of the symbolic (logical, orderly)
aspect of communication that is none other than the law of the father.
Accordingly, the literary critic, Jacqueline Rose, writes:

> Kristeva has ... been attractive to feminism because of the way that she
> exposes the complacent identities of psycho-sexual life. But as soon as we try
> to draw out of that exposure an image of femininity which escapes the strait-
> jacket of symbolic forms, we fall straight into that essentialism and primacy of
> the semiotic which is one of the most problematic aspects of her work.
>
> (as quoted in Oliver 1993a: 53)

The criticism of the American philosopher Nancy Fraser is less subtle:

> [D]espite [Kristeva's] explicit criticisms of gynocentrism, there is a strand of
> her thought that implicitly partakes of it – I mean Kristeva's quasi-biologistic,
> essentializing identification of women's femininity with maternity. Maternity,
> for her, is the way that women, as opposed to men, touch base with the pre-
> Oedipal, semiotic residue. (Men do it by writing avant-garde poetry; women do
> it by having babies.) Here Kristeva dehistoricizes and psychologizes mother-
> hood, conflating conception, pregnancy, birthing, nursing, and childrearing,
> abstracting all of them from sociopolitical context, and erecting her own essen-
> tialist stereotype of femininity.
>
> (1992: 190)

In this passage, Fraser faults Kristeva for being essentialist, and here
clearly she has biological essentialism in mind. But Fraser also notes
another, seemingly opposite, theme in Kristeva's work. Fraser writes

SEX AND GENDER

Many feminists find it useful to distinguish the biological category of sex –
i.e. of male and female – from the cultural category of gender. The idea here
is that masculinity and femininity are social and cultural constructions,
whereas being male or female is a biological fact (though with modern
medicine certainly amenable to change). This is why we can think of some
biological men as rather feminine or some women as masculine. Genders
"float" and can attach themselves to different sexes. Many "gender theorists" find this category of gender useful, because it helps explain how
cultural and sexist stereotypes arose and how they can be changed. Even
if it were true that "biology is destiny," certainly cultural constructions are
not so predetermined and unchangeable.

that Kristeva "reverses herself and recoils from her construct, insisting
that 'women' do not exist, that feminine identity is fictitious, and that
feminist movements therefore tend toward the religious and the proto-
totalitarian" (ibid.). Fraser is clearly mystified, writing: "she ends up
alternating essentialist gynocentric moments with anti-essentialist
nominalistic moments, moments that consolidate an ahistorical, undifferentiated, maternal feminine gender identity with moments that
repudiate women's identities altogether" (ibid.).

Is Kristeva truly so schizophrenic? Or is Fraser missing something?
Fraser seems to be trying to understand Kristeva's texts with the handy
tool of the sex/gender distinction. Fraser is drawing a parallel between
Kristeva's semiotic/symbolic distinction and the feminist sex/gender
distinction.

Tina Chanter describes the "unspoken feminist commitment to the
ideology of sex and gender" as follows:

> The story that feminism tells itself is a story in which gender plays the lead
> role. Once we realized that femininity was culturally constructed, and not
> inscribed in our natures, we could change the ways in which gender was
> constructed. Since we can transform culture, whatever natural differences
> distinguish the sexes become insignificant. In effect, then, sex, nature, biology,
> and bodies are written out of the feminist picture. What is important for
> feminism is gender, culture, society, and history.

(1993: 185)

As Chanter argues, Kristeva's critics find fault with Kristeva by mapping the feminist distinction between sex and gender onto Kristeva's distinction between the semiotic and the symbolic, equating the semiotic aspect of signification with biological, including sexual, processes and the symbolic with culturally-defined gender. Chanter argues that, to the contrary, Kristeva's work unsettles the sex/gender dichotomy: the semiotic rhythms and charges are part of our signifying practices. So, we cannot mark a tidy break between bodies and culture, making it impossible to siphon off gender from sex.

Let me add that the sex/gender distinction sets the pair up in opposition: we are *either* going to talk about femininity (or masculinity) as a sexual-bodily-biological-determinist matter *or* as a cultural-linguistic-provisional construction. Kristeva's notions of semiotic and symbolic operate quite differently. The two are both moments, always present, in the discourse of speaking beings. Someone might try to stand here before you and speak as logically and methodically as possible, but the semiotic aspects of signification will have their way. Insofar as a speaking being is embodied and desiring, that is, *alive*, her attempts at purely logical discourse will always be disrupted. While the critics worry that any talk of biological processes is essentialist, people's embodiedness will always have its say.

Kristeva's critics argue that her notion of the semiotic prediscursively naturalizes femininity. In other words, it makes women's femininity a biological fact and not a cultural construction. Thus, they argue, her theory collapses into biological essentialism. As Kelly Oliver and other defenders of Kristeva's work have pointed out, this charge is inaccurate, because the semiotic operates discursively after the speaking being enters language. Kristeva's defenders have shown that Kristeva does not locate biological processes prior to, or anterior to, culture and language, so her theory is not, properly speaking, essentialist. Insofar as the body is mediated through language, it becomes a cultural construction as well.

Though sound, this defense may not fully satisfy the critics; they are averse to any discussion of female biology. This aversion seems to have its roots in an implicit acceptance of the fundamental presupposition of the founding father of modern philosophy, René Descartes (1596–1650): that the true self is a mind and not a body, a "thinking thing" and not a physical thing (an "extended substance"). The Cartesian dualism of two substances, with mind over matter, sets up human nature as being essentially mind, as being the glassy essence whose job is to perceive essence, the ground for all knowledge, the possibility of representing the world. As a consequence of this dualism, anything that evoked extended substance – biological processes, emotion, the body, etc. – was seen as incapable of taking part in the great project of the modern era, to further human knowledge. Hence, women seem to be fated to being people whose essence was bodily; they are unable to realize the ideal of being *res cogitans* – a thinking thing. Women have historically been identified with their bodies and thus seen, in the history of philosophy, more as extended rather than as thinking things. To the extent that women are equated with their bodies, they are put on the wrong end of the Cartesian map of human identity.

With regard to subjectivity, Cartesian dualism postulates two substances – one essential to being, the other not. For women to be assigned to bodies ties them essentially to being beings without essences. The problem then is not essentialism but a metaphysics that makes women disappear. No wonder that so many feminists shun metaphysics; seemingly, it bodes only ill for women. When a Cartesian framework is presupposed, no feminist in her right mind would talk about women's bodies. Understandably, then, many feminists have bristled at Kristeva's valorization of the undeniably *bodily* experience of maternity, especially in two key essays, "Women's Time" and "Stabat Mater."

"STABAT MATER"

In 1977, the journal *Tel Quel* published an essay by Kristeva titled "Hérethique de l'amour." For the title, Kristeva coined the word *hérethique* by joining the French word for heretical (*hérétique*) with the word for ethics (*éthique*). The result is *hérethique*, so the original title could be translated as "the heretical ethics of love." The English translation of the essay, published in *Tales of Love* (1987) is titled with the Latin phrase, "Stabat Mater," which refers to a hymn about the Virgin Mary's agony during Christ's crucifixion: the hymn begins, "*Stabat mater dolorosa*," meaning "Stood the Mother, full of grief" (Kristeva 1986: 160). In this essay, Kristeva describes maternity both from the point of view of being a mother and of representing maternity. Much of the essay is presented in two columns, parallel discussions written in entirely different registers. In the left-hand column of the essay,

Kristeva writes very poetically, relating how, in her own pregnancy (at least so we are led to believe), she experienced herself as both rational and desiring, as seeking jouissance, as knowing a profound love for this "other" within, who was not really an other but a part of herself. She found that the distinction between self and other blurs in the experience of pregnancy. And the wonder of giving birth is that what was once a part of oneself now becomes other, but never entirely. One acts for this other neither out of altruism or selfishness or duty/law.

As Kristeva writes, apparently drawing from her own experience, the infant is protected by the mother, nourished by her body, soothed by her flesh and her voice. And the mother too is taken in and over by her near unity and imminent division of and from this child. The relationship between mother and the unborn and newborn child begins prior to language. But, for the newborn to attain subjectivity, it will have to learn language, submit to "the Law," etc. But it will not relinquish its desire to transgress the Law.

In the right-hand column, written more prosaically, Kristeva discusses representations of maternity and the functions these serve:

> Man overcomes the unthinkable of death by postulating maternal love in its place – in the place and stead of death and thought. This love . . . psychologically is perhaps a recall . . . of the primal shelter that insured the survival of the newborn.

> (Kristeva 1987: 252)

In other words, man needs a representation of maternal love in order to deal with our mortality. I should note that the "man" Kristeva is primarily pointing to in this passage is the Italian composer of *Stabat Mater*, Giovanni Battista Pergolesi (1710–1736), who died of tuberculosis when he was only twenty-six. Perhaps his fantasy of the virgin's maternal love covered over his own anguish of dying. He could not live well with the thought of death unless he also had a thought of a mother's plentiful love. This fantasy seems to be at the root of the dominant representation of motherhood, a representation held up by men and, it seems, implicitly adopted by most women who become mothers. The representation calls for women's sublimation of their desires, their asceticism, and, ultimately, masochism.

Kristeva laments that psychoanalytic thought has offered little toward a way out of this representation of women, for women:

In simplified fashion, the only thing Freud tells us concerning motherhood is that the desire for a child is a transformation of either penis envy or anal drive, and this allows her to discover the neurotic equation child-penis-feces. We are thus enlightened concerning an essential aspect of male phantasmatics with respect to childbirth, and female phantasmatics as well, to the extent that it embraces, in large part and in its hysterical labyrinths, the male one.

(ibid.: 254–255)

In other words, Freud only tried to understand the existing trope of motherhood, not to change it. "The fact remains, as far as the complexities and pitfalls of maternal experience are involved, that Freud offers only a massive *nothing*, which, for those who might analyze it, is punctuated with this or that remark on the part of Freud's mother" (ibid.: 255). Playing on Freud's quip that woman was a dark continent, an unknown, Kristeva writes: "There thus remained for his followers an entire continent to explore, a black one indeed" (ibid.). But Freud's followers shed no light, as far as Kristeva sees; so she suggests:

There might doubtless be a way to approach the dark area that motherhood constitutes for a woman; one needs to listen, more carefully than ever, to what mothers are saying today, through their economic difficulties and, beyond the guilt that a too existentialist feminism handed down, through their discomforts, insomnias, joys, angers, desires, pains, and pleasures.

(ibid.: 256)

Contemporary women still want to be mothers, but they do not want to be self-abnegating masochists, and, given that the representation of motherhood calls on them to renounce their own desires, modern women who choose motherhood seem to be in a bind. Kristeva wants to find a way out of this problem that does not call for women to choose between motherhood and their own desires, but that, instead, reconstitutes our representation of motherhood. The difficulty, though, is that the experience of pregnancy, labor, birth, and maternity is in fact wrenching and painful. It does in fact blur the borders of self-hood, posing a kind of cataclysm for a woman who has been, until then, comfortably situated in the symbolic:

The unspoken doubtless weighs first on the maternal body: as no signifier can uplift it without leaving a remainder, for the signifier is always meaning, communication, or structure, whereas a woman as mother would be, instead, a strange fold that changes culture into nature, the speaking into biology. Although it concerns every woman's body, the heterogeneity that cannot be subsumed in the signifier nevertheless explodes violently with pregnancy (the threshold of culture and nature) and the child's arrival (which extracts woman out of her oneness and gives her the possibility – but not the certainty – of reaching out to the other, the ethical). Those particularities of the maternal body compose woman into a being of folds, a catastrophe of being.

(ibid.: 259–260)

Yet, even as pregnancy and labor destabilize women's symbolic position, the experience is gratifying because it gives women a way to be the "ultimate guarantee of society, without which society will not reproduce and will not maintain a constancy of standardized household" (ibid.: 260). The difficulty Kristeva articulates is to find a way to represent motherhood as fulfilling without being masochistic:

Feminine perversion [*père-version*, a play on the French word for father] is coiled up in the desire for law as desire for reproduction and continuity; it promotes feminine masochism to the rank of structure stabilizer (against its deviations); by assuring the mother that she may thus enter into an order that is above humans' will it gives her her reward of pleasure.

(ibid.: 260)

Unfortunately, at the end of the essay Kristeva points the way very sketchily. And what she writes is provocative. She calls for an analysis and understanding that will "lead to an acknowledgment of what is irreducible, of the irreconcilable interest of both sexes in asserting their differences, in the quest of each one – and of women, after all – for an appropriate fulfillment" (ibid.: 262).

Many readers have found in this essay ample reason to think that Kristeva is an essentialist, taking as she does the experience of motherhood as so important and potentially fulfilling. At first glance she may seem to be committing the sin of biological essentialism, equating women with their bodies and the biological function of bearing children, denying the importance of their symbolic signifying practice. But when read closer, she appears to defy the usual framework that reduces women to their bodies.

Instead of taking culture and nature as mutually exclusive terms, she sees that they can be folded into one another – via the maternal body. Our symbolic language tries to signify neatly, to capture truth without a remainder, but the experience of pregnancy and mothering shatters this attempt. A pregnant women who has otherwise been an established member of the symbolic community may find herself heeding her biology minutely. Where before she could parade as an individual, affirming her culture's individualistic ethos, now she is undeniably at least two. While her other ethical relationships could have been treated as exchanges based upon symmetrical and universal duty between individuals, she now will have a relationship with someone who is neither strictly self nor other.

Everyone, being born of mothers, will have some archaic knowledge of this, whether this love was given well or miserly. In Kristeva's view, maternal love performs a crucial function:

> Now, if a contemporary ethics is no longer seen as being the same as morality; if ethics amounts to not avoiding the embarrassing and inevitable problematics of the law but giving it flesh, language, and jouissance – in that case its reformulation demands the contribution of women. Of women who harbor the desire to reproduce (to have stability). Of women who are available so that our speaking species, which knows it is mortal, might withstand death. Of mothers. For an heretical ethics separated from morality, an *herethics*, is perhaps no more than that which in life makes bonds, thoughts, and therefore the thought of death, bearable: herethics is undeath [*a-mort*], love.
>
> (1987: 262–263)

Kristeva's mention of this new kind of ethics is tantalizing but brief. She mentions it here and in a few other places, but never discusses it extensively. Kelly Oliver calls it an "outlaw ethics," saying:

> [it is] founded on the ambiguity in pregnancy and birth between subject and object positions. It is an ethics that challenges rather than presupposes an autonomous ethical agent. Herethics sets up one's obligations to the other as obligations to the self and obligations to the species. This ethics binds the subject to the other through love and not Law. . . . [T]he model of ethical love is the mother's love for the child, which is a love for herself and a love for her own mother. The mother's love is also the willingness to give herself up, to embrace the strangeness within herself.
>
> (1993: 183)

With the neologism, *herethics*, Kristeva is calling for an ethics that is not just about the love between mother and child. It is about something much larger: finding a bridge between the semiotic and the symbolic. As the philosopher, Alison Ainley, writes:

> [Kristeva] seems to be suggesting that the location of ethical practice should no longer lie in the reformulation and attempted perfection of rules and laws. Instead, the disruptive effect of the subject in process/on trial as it is worked out in Kristeva's theorization points toward a different trajectory of the ethical subject. The constant transgression and renewal of the subject's positioning with regard to the process of signification *reinserts* such a subject into the transformation of community and discourse. As a consequence it seems it is the boundaries at which transformations are taking place and new practices are being forged where the focus of attention should lie.
>
> (1990: 55)

According to Ainley, Kristeva "suggests that the site of motherhood gains its subversive potential as 'the threshold of nature and culture,' the woman who is both *mother*, guarantor of the community and *other*, 'the polymorphic, orgasmic body, laughing and desiring'" (ibid.: 58).

Ainley is right to point to how the semiotic and transgressive aspects of the speaking being disrupts the law, but Kristeva thinks the symbolic and law-abiding aspect of being a speaking being is vital as well. Otherwise, subjectivity – as delineating myself from an other – would be impossible. Kristeva's ethics calls for finding a way for us to have subjectivity via the law and the symbolic without having to fight off the semiotic. This seems to be about undoing the dualisms of mind/ body, culture/nature, and word/flesh. The mother–child relationship suggests a way to undo these dualisms; the mother does right for her child not just out of duty (law) but out of love, a love that is not just for an other but for what was once in her and for the species, for the singular other and for the universal. (Note how this love surpasses the dichotomy between egoism and altruism.) By heeding the experience of maternity, Kristeva argues, we can give birth to this new ethics.

KRISTEVA'S PROCESS PHILOSOPHY

So, we need mothers. Again, this might seem essentialist, good fuel for conservatives. But Kristeva does not make generalizations about

METAPHYSICS AND ONTOLOGY

Metaphysics is a branch of philosophy that studies the ultimate nature of reality, the reality that cannot be observed the way that the objects of physics can be observed. (This makes the study "meta" physical – beyond the physical.) Ontology is a subset of metaphysics. It is the study of the existence or "being" of things.

women themselves. In her poetic column she is giving a first-person account of a mother's experience. In the right-hand column she is discussing symbolic representations, not women per se. And her own view is hardly conservative. The function of motherhood depicted here is radical: to be a fold between nature and culture, self and other, life and death, a fold that is a catastrophe of being that shatters the usual representations. I read "catastrophe" here as meaning not an end or cataclysm but "an event that produces a subversion of the usual order of things."

Moreover, Kristeva is not calling for, as some critics have put it, "compulsory maternity," that it be a woman's duty to bear children. Yes, the women who do bear children are providing a gift to humanity, ensuring our survival. Kristeva's main point is that we need a better way of thinking, a new representation of motherhood. The Virgin Mary won't do.

In my reading of her work, Kristeva is offering a representation based upon a metaphysics radically different from the "substance ontology" of Cartesian metaphysics (the view that the primary category of being is a substance or thing). I see her working out of another metaphysical tradition, a *process philosophy* that perhaps originated with the pre-Socratic philosopher, Heraclitus (circa 500 BC) and is now associated with the English philosopher, Alfred North Whitehead (1861–1947). But it is also an approach central to the continental philosophies of Friedrich Nietzsche (1844–1900), Martin Heidegger (1889–1976), and Gilles Deleuze (1925–1995). All these philosophers share an approach to metaphysics that defies the central role that substance has played. Process philosophy is not a system of philosophy; it has no strict tenets; rather, the term captures a style of metaphysical inquiry that emphasizes events rather than substance. Standard metaphysics emphasizes substance, essence, fixity, persistence, identity, and continuity. It seeks the essence that can survive the comings and goings of accidents: what persists through time. Process metaphysics emphasizes change, event, novelty, activity, and fluidity. Process philosophers think that *what things are* is in flux. Whatever is is always changing rather than persisting. The answer to the ancient Greek question, *To ti einai?* (What is this?), is less a substrate or matter than perhaps a code or script. Perhaps what is is not a thing (substance) but a pattern of change, a process.

To my knowledge, Kristeva never explicitly identifies herself as a process philosopher, though, no doubt, if the question were put to her she would say that she is, for all her key terms – from the subject in process to the *chora* to abjection and transference love – invoke movement, change, and dynamism. It is also evident in her choice of psychoanalytic models. Instead of adopting a model of ego psychology and the realist ego (based upon Freud's "second topology" of ego, id, and superego), Kristeva draws on Lacan's model, which draws from Freud's earlier theory of the narcissistic ego. The theories of the realist ego and ego psychology hold that the ego is a substance of sorts, which implies that the ego is a fixed entity. Alternatively, a Freudian-libidinal model suggests that the ego evolves. In his essay on narcissism, Freud suggests a hydraulic model of the ego, where the "shape" of the ego is simply the shape and degree of its libidinal investments, whether in itself (ego-libido) or in others (object-libido).

From a Kristevan point of view, language is both a biological and a cultural process by which the speaking subject constitutes history and society. Kristeva says she holds "the dramatic notion of language as a risky practice, allowing the speaking animal to sense the rhythm of the body as well as the upheavals of history" (1980: 34). For Kristeva, subjectivity originates with the drives and processes that psychoanalytic theory describes. Even after subjectivity arises, it is never a stable, fixed entity. In her words, it is an open system. Drawing on Freud's narcissistic model of libidinal energy in cathexis, Kristeva argues that the psyche, as an open system, is the shape of its attachments. This does not mean that subjectivity arises *ex nihilo*. There is an origin, though this origin is not a substance; it is a movement. Recall that the *chora* denotes "an essentially mobile and extremely provisional articulation constituted by movements and their ephemeral stases" (Kristeva 1984: 25). The term *chora* represents

> a *disposition* that already depends on representation. ... Although our theo-
> retical description of the *chora* is itself part of the discourse of representation
> that offers it as evidence, the *chora*, as rupture and articulations (rhythm),
> precedes evidence, verisimilitude, spatiality, and temporality.

> (ibid.: 26)

Clearly there is a fold in Kristeva's work between culture and bodies, what others might call gender and sex. In some essays it is the maternal body. But in many others it is simply the speaking being, a person who happens to have been born into a network of relationships, kin, language, and law, who must negotiate these as well as the knowledge of her or his own coming death. So this speaking being has many passages to negotiate, and is a fold in them all. Where other process philosophers might be content to identify these folds, events, movements, and other assorted catastrophes of being, Kristeva also wants to ease the passage. This I think motivates her work not only as a philosopher, but as a psychoanalyst.

In her own psychoanalytic practice, Kristeva takes the analytic experience as a process of heeding the folds and reconfiguring the relationship between bodies and culture. As she says in *Sens et non-sens de la révolte* (*The Sense and Non-sense of Revolt*):

> I want to emphasize the copresence of sexuality and thought in order to dis-
> sociate myself from two currents of thought that investigate the psyche:
> cognitivism, on the one hand, which considers the mind solely from the point
> of view of consciousness, and a pre-Lacanian psychoanalysis, on the other.
> ... Instead of psychoanalysis as a matheme of the signifier, or a theory of
> "the mind," or the transaction of organs and drives, I will try to show that the
> originality of the Freudian discovery resides in this: psychoanalysis is a clinic
> and a theory of the copresence of the development of thought *and* of sexuality.
> This two-sided (thought/sexuality) approach to the speaking being, which I see
> at the heart of the analytical experience, is an original variant of the age-old
> notion of dualism, and far from biologizing the essence of man, it centers the
> study of the psychical apparatus, its deployment, and its obstacles, in the bi-
> univocal dependency of thought-sexuality/sexuality-thought. As language is
> the domain of this interaction, it is here that Freud found the "other scene," that
> of the unconscious, with its components (representatives of the drives) and its
> logic (primary processes) irreducible to conscious linguistic communication.

> (2000: 94–95)

In other words, psychoanalysis is a way of listening for and to both thought and sexuality. Language is the site of this interaction, but the interaction is never reducible to language. So it would be a mistake to try to siphon language and culture off from bodies as some feminist critics want to siphon gender off from sex. In the psychoanalytic setting, our minds and bodies, culture and biological processes are inextricable. The analysand's speech renders her naked, giving lie to any attempt in other settings to set off civilization from desire. So we could take the analytic setting as paradigmatic, as the bare bones of what speaking beings reveal when they speak.

What is revealed is that the self is not mappable onto a Cartesian scheme of substance, that is, onto an exclusionary distinction between bodily beings and thinking beings. The analysand's language folds biology and culture. Bodies come into play in the signifying process, but signification can never be reduced to bodies. As a folding, language is a process. As a process, it undoes any essentialist notion that the self is a mind apart from a body. So Kristeva's talk of bodies, of the semiotic, of sexuality cannot be reduced, as Fraser and other critics would have it, to being essentialist. What could this essence be? Instead of a reduction, we find in Kristeva's work an explosion of the old categories.

SUMMARY

In adopting a process understanding of biology and the drives and seeing the self as a fluid, mobile, subject in process Kristeva disables or at least displaces the charge of essentialism. Despite feminist concerns that Kristeva is an essentialist, Kristeva's philosophy invokes a metaphysics of process rather than substance and is thus fundamentally incompatible with essentialism. Feminism in Kristeva's philosophy could be seen as an attempt to resist the essentialism that would exclude all that is mobile and vital. In this sense, woman is not identified with the semiotic *chora*; rather, feminists can use the semiotic *chora* strategically to signify a sexual difference in which contingency, history, and transformation occur.

6

WOMEN'S TIME

Kristeva's interest in sexual difference sets her apart from an earlier generation of feminists where "difference" was something to be overcome, not championed. These were the trailblazers of the Enlightenment, the suffragists of the nineteenth century, and the advocates for equal rights and freedom of the twentieth century. They fought for a gamut of rights, from the right to vote to the right to control one's own body – which translates into reproductive freedom. For the most part, this early feminism sought to show that women deserved all the same rights and privileges that men had been accorded. To support this claim they emphasized women's similarity to men and minimized the differences.

After many of this early generation's goals were won, a new kind of feminism emerged, one that sought to highlight and appreciate women's uniqueness. At first glance, Kristeva's feminism might seem to be of this sort. But she is very clear about distinguishing herself from this group:

> Certain feminists, in France particularly, say that whatever is in language is of the order of strict designation, of understanding, of logic, and it is male. Ultimately, theory or science is phallic, is male. On the other hand that which is feminine in language is whatever has to do with the imprecise, with the whisper, with impulses, perhaps with primary processes, with rhetoric – in

other words, speaking roughly, the domain of literary expression, the region of the tacit, the vague, to which one would escape from the too-tight tailoring of the linguistic sign and of logic.

(Guberman 1996: 116)

Kristeva's choice of words shows that she certainly does not embrace this approach. It is, she says:

a Manichean position that consists in designating as feminine a phase or a modality in the functioning of language. And if one assigns women that phase alone, this in fact amounts to maintaining women in a position of inferiority, and, in any case, of marginality, to reserving for them the lace of the childish, of the unsayable, or of the hysteric.

(Guberman 1996: 116–117)

Kristeva thinks that this second approach can certainly serve a subversive function – but at too great a cost to women's capacities.

More than twenty-five years ago, when American feminists were still trying (in vain) to pass an equal rights amendment to the US Constitution, Kristeva noted these two distinct tracks that feminist movements have taken: (1) to infiltrate the social order; and (2) to try to subvert it. In an interview first published in 1975, she observed that, having been placed in a subordinate position to power and language, women have tried both these options:

Even though she is excluded from power and language, she possesses the hidden, invisible element that allows them to function. On the one hand, she can become a source of negativity and harassment, pushing power to its limits and then struggling with it. This is the classic role of the hysteric, who runs the risk of exploding into a symptom that is revolutionary in the positive and constructive sense of the word. Yet she can also lay claim to power until she identifies with it and supplants it. One might wonder if some aspects of the feminist agenda do not fail because they attempt to identify with power. Such attempts make women into a counterpower filling gaps in official power – or into a promised land consisting of an ultimately harmonious society believed to consist only of women who know the truth about the mysteries of an imaginary society lacking any internal contradiction.

(ibid.: 105–106)

Kristeva calls this kind of feminist thinking a "phantasmatic cohesion." She seems to prefer the first tactic: woman as the vigilant outsider. But she is also critical of feminist movements that wish to permanently situate women in this marginal position.

Both approaches are understandable and useful to an extent, Kristeva suggests. But clearly she thinks there must be some other approach as well. She begins to sketch out this third way in an essay she wrote a year after "Stabat Mater," "Le Temps des femmes," which was translated and published in English as "Women's Time" in 1981. She updated it slightly and republished it in her 1993 book, *Nouvelles maladies de l'âme*, which was published in English as *New Maladies of the Soul*. In the words of the feminist scholar, Toril Moi: "From a feminist perspective, this is one of Kristeva's most important essays, not least because she here explicitly addresses the question of feminism and its relations to femininity on the one hand, and the symbolic order on the other" (Kristeva 1986: 187).

FEMINISM'S GENERATIONS

In "Women's Time," she notes three "generations" of European feminism. By generation she means "less a chronology than a *signifying* space, a mental space that is at once corporeal and desirous" (Kristeva 1995: 222) – in other words, a particular approach or attitude. The first generation, which she primarily locates prior to 1968, was the movement in which women sought all the same rights and prerogatives that men had. This was the movement that called for equal rights and equal treatment. Its central tenet was that women deserved such things because really they were "just like" men. There were no truly important differences between the sexes, so they should be treated the same. This first generation of women activists sought to inhabit the same "time" that men had inhabited: the time of linear history, where women's accomplishments could be inserted in the linear timeline of human history. These women argued that women "must appropriate the logical, mastering scientific, theoretical apparatus" and they "consider it extremely gratifying that there are women physicists, theorists, and philosophers. In saying this," Kristeva notes, "they preserve for women an extremely important place in the domain of culture" (Guberman 1996: 117). Previously, culture's public, linear time had only been available to men. Women inhabited the household, where

FATHER'S TIME, MOTHER'S SPECIES

In "Women's Time," Kristeva borrows James Joyce's phrase, "father's time, mother's species," to designate two dimensions that human beings have occupied. "Father's time" refers to the linear time that men have inhabited, with its sense of history, destiny, and progress. The phrase "mother's species" evokes the realm that women have traditionally occupied: a space that generates the human species, a space like the *chora*, where time is marked by repetition on the one hand and a sense of the eternity of the species on the other.

the time that ruled was cyclical, as in the time – again – for cooking or cleaning or birthing or sleeping. In the realm of the household, time moves in a circle. Nothing new really is created – that would be production – instead the old is recreated or reproduced. The first generation of feminists wanted out of circular time and into the history-making possibility of linear time.

The first generation of feminists repudiated anything that made them different from men and sought instead to identify with the male, symbolic order. This made them, oddly enough, quite accepting of the status quo:

> When the women's movement began as the struggle of suffragists and exis-tential feminists, it sought to stake out its place in the linear time of planning and history. As a result, although the movement was universalist from the start, it was deeply rooted in the sociopolitical life of nations. The political demands of women, their struggles for equal pay for equal work and for the right to the same opportunities as men have, as well as the rejection of feminine or maternal traits considered incompatible with participation in such a history all stem from the logic of identification with values that are not ideological (such values have been rightly criticized as too reactionary) but logical and ontolog-ical with regard to the dominant rationality of the nation and the state.
>
> (Kristeva 1995: 207)

The first generation of feminists identified with and upheld the existing order. It didn't want to overturn the system. It wanted to join it. It wanted all the rights accorded to men – plus the right to reproductive freedom. Kristeva lauds the accomplishments made in these areas, as do most feminists who have succeeded the first generation. What sets the subsequent generations apart, though, is their recognition that the struggle to "join" the old boys' club by way of identifying with it will only go so far.

THE LIMITS OF THE SYSTEM

As an important and telling example, Kristeva points to the gains made in socialist Eastern Europe (recall that she is writing during the reign of Soviet and Eastern-bloc communism). In many respects, socialism is the height of the egalitarian ideal, which developed in the eighteenth-century movement known as the Enlightenment. Operating, as it does, "in the spirit of the egalitarian and universalist context of Enlightenment humanism," socialism adheres to the idea "that identity between the sexes is the only way to liberate 'the second sex'" (Kristeva 1995: 209). So, one would think that women could have "had it all" under socialism. For those feminists acting in a time and place where socialism was a promising frontier, if not already a reality, it would seem to make eminent sense to try to join the old boys' club. For the most part, this was a good strategy: "in Eastern Europe, various blunders and vacillations have not prevented three of the most important demands of the early feminist movement from being answered to: the demands of economic, political, and professional equality" (ibid.: 210).

But one demand was not forthcoming: the demand for sexual equality, as Kristeva puts it, though she seems to have in mind sexual freedom, the sexual freedom tied to a recognition of women's particular desires and needs. For the state to grant women this freedom would have required, for one, "permissiveness in sexual relationships as well as abortion and contraceptive rights" (ibid.). This demand remained "inhibited by a certain Marxist ethics as well as by the reason of state" (ibid.). Acceding to the demand would also have required that socialism acknowledge the difference and particularity of women, but, built as it is on Enlightenment ideals of "universality," socialism could not appreciate women's particularity, much less women's desires. All this is to say that the first generation's strategy simply would not work here, because the issue of sexual equality was bound up with the underlying sexual and symbolic contract. In other words, *it was the logic of the overall system itself* that denied women sexual equality. Women would never gain sexual freedom by identifying with the system. Kristeva's point would apply to any advanced society, liberal as well as socialist. Her point was not to denigrate socialism, but to say that – no matter how ideal – any system positions its members in different ways. "Sexual, biological, physiological, and reproductive difference reflects a difference in the relation between subjects and the symbolic contract – that is, the social contract" (ibid.).

In a 1980 interview, Kristeva noted that women's protest must be more than a fight for recognitions of rights. Women's protest, she said:

> is a protest that consists in demanding that attention be paid to the subjective particularity that an individual represents in the social order, of course, but also and above all in relation to what essentially differentiates that individual, which is the individual's sexual difference. How can one define this sexual difference? It is not solely biological; it is, above all, given in the representations that we ourselves make of this difference. We have no other means of constructing this representation than through language, through tools for symbolizing.

(Guberman 1996: 116)

Kristeva is arguing that it is not just biological differences that differentiate women from men. Even these differences have to be *articulated* to be meaningful. It is the symbolic realm that differentiates the sexes. Seeing the social order and the symbolic order as two dimensions of a large system (the psychosymbolic structure), Kristeva argues that women's demands cannot be met by identifying with the system or by asking the system to identify with them.

THE SECOND GENERATION: DIFFERENCE FEMINISM

This structural fact began to dawn on the generation that came after 1968. Understanding this structure has been "a matter of clarifying the difference between men and women as concerns their respective relationships to power, language, and meaning" (Kristeva 1995: 210). Many in this generation turned to psychoanalytic theory to glean the insight (discussed in Chapter 1) that the symbolic order is founded upon a castration anxiety or fear. Kristeva cites Freud's observation that "castration is an imaginary construction" that moves a person from an imaginary plenitude to a region of lack or desire, the very lack that sets the symbolic field in motion. The sociosymbolic field, then, is founded on this imagined "cut." In general, men respond to this fear by glorifying "this separation and language while trying, petrified as they are, to master them." Women are positioned as beings constituted by a lack (imagined castration) that propels them into the symbolic realm in search, however vain, of satisfaction. Imagined castration forces women to leave the imaginary realm of plenitude for the social-symbolic order.

These and other insights helped the second generation see what women have had to sacrifice in order to uphold the social contract:

> At the interior of this psychosymbolic structure, women feel rejected from language and the social bond, in which they discover neither the affects nor the meanings of the relationships they enjoy with nature, their bodies, their children's bodies, another woman, or a man. The accompanying frustration, which is also experienced by some men, is the quintessence of the new feminist ideology. Consequently, it is difficult, if not impossible, for women to adhere to the sacrificial logic of separation and syntactic links upon which language and the social code are based, and this can eventually lead to a rejection of the symbolic that is experienced as a rejection of the paternal function and may result in psychosis.
>
> (ibid.: 213)

The second generation began to see that, at the heart of a sexist society, was a psychosymbolic structure that called for separation – between signs and their meanings as well as between people. Unwilling to accept such losses, many women of the second generation have decided to revolt against the sacrificial logic of this contract.

Where the first generation minimized difference, the second generation of European feminists began to focus on it intently, often simply by revaluing what the old system devalued: all that is womanly. On the whole, Kristeva characterizes the second, post-1968 generation of feminism as follows: it was not and still is not willing to accommodate the existing system. Composed of women influenced by psychoanalytic thought and the arts, the second generation "is characterized by a quasi-universal rejection of linear temporality and by a highly pronounced mistrust of political life" (ibid.: 208). While it continues to call for the kinds of gains the first generation sought, "it sees itself in a different light" and seeks a language for women's "corporeal and intersubjective experiences, which have been silenced by the cultures of the past" (ibid.). Turning away from the first generation's interest in linear time, the second generation has sought to return to women's archaic, cyclical time, as well as to the "monumental" time of the species. Instead of seeking to be producers in a linear history, they have sought ways to revalue the lives of women as upholders of the species. "Today, feminism is returning to an archaic (mythic) memory as well as to the cyclical or monumental temporality of marginal movements" (ibid.).

In various texts and interviews, Kristeva draws on a passage from Hegel to describe what she finds very promising in the second generation's approach. She refers to a passage in his *Phenomenology of Spirit* (first published in 1807), in which Hegel describes women, namely the fictional woman, Antigone, the protagonist of a play by the same name written by the Greek playwright, Sophocles (495–406 BC), as "the eternal irony of the community" (1977: 288). Evoking Hegel, Kristeva said in a 1989 interview:

> I am very attached to the idea of the woman as irrecuperable foreigner. But I know that certain American feminists do not think well of such an idea, because they want a positivist notion of woman. But one can be positive by starting with this permanent marginality, which is the motor of change. So I think that for me femininity is exactly this lunar form, in the way that the moon is the inverse of the sun of our identity. From this point of view, perhaps we women have it more than the men, but the men have it also. And to try to preserve this part as unreconcilable permits us perhaps always to be what Hegel called the eternal irony of the community. That is to say, a sort of separate vigilance that keeps groups from closing up, from becoming homogeneous and so oppressive. That is, I see the role of women as a sort of vigilance, a strangeness, as always to be on guard and contestatory.
>
> (Guberman 1996: 45)

Kristeva likes the moments when women can play this role. But they are rare, she thinks, because most women are too entranced by the image of woman as mother and by respect for the paternal law to be free to remain in the margins subverting or deriding the law.

Where the first generation spurned the activity of mothering (which had historically relegated women to the household) in favor of activity in the linear time of the public sphere, the second generation has re-embraced mothering:

> The majority of women today feel that they have a mission to put a child into the world. This brings up a question for the new generation that the preceding one repudiated: what lies behind this desire to be a mother? Unable to answer this question, feminist ideology opens the door to a return of religion, which may serve to pacify anxiety, suffering, and maternal expectations.
>
> (Kristeva 1995: 219)

To the extent that the second generation embraces the role of motherhood, it risks becoming another religion. Instead of God, it has "Woman" and "Her power." The second generation's return to mothering presents a problem insofar as it is seen as a way to recuperate women's archaic and mythic memory. Kristeva sees in this second generation a tendency to equate the "good substance" that women supposedly tap into with this myth of the archaic mother. One danger here is that actual women in their uniqueness, individuality, and particularity are lost under the monolith of Woman.

Another danger is more serious: the danger of holding up the myth of the mother as a cure for the ills of the psychosymbolic order. "Eternal debt toward the mother has made her more vulnerable to the symbolic order, more fragile when she suffers from it, and more virulent when she protects herself" (ibid.: 218). This contrast between the mythic mother and the sociosymbolic order has been used to justify violence against the system:

> If the archetypal belief in a good and sound chimerical substance is essentially a belief in the omnipotence of an archaic, fulfilled, complete, all-encompassing mother who is not frustrated, not separated, and who lacks the "cut" that permits symbolism (that is, who lacks castration), the ensuing violence would be impossible to defuse without challenging the very myth of the archaic mother.
>
> (ibid.: 218)

While the second generation's revolt against the established order is understandable, it is dangerous and potentially lethal. Sometimes, "by fighting against evil, we reproduce it, this time at the core of the social bond – the bond between men and women" (ibid.: 214). Kristeva notes the ways in which

> various feminist currents . . . reject the powers that be and make the second sex into a *countersociety*, a sort of alter ego of official society that harbors hopes

> for pleasure. This female society can be opposed to the sacrificial and frus-
> trating sociosymbolic contract: a countersociety imagined to be harmonious,
> permissive, free, and blissful.
>
> (ibid.: 215)

The imagined countersociety preserves itself as such by expelling what it deems to be responsible for evil. It thinks of itself as containing some "good substance" that it opposes to a "guilty party." This scapegoat could be "the foreigner, money, another religion, or the other sex" (ibid.: 216).

Doesn't this logic, Kristeva asks, lead to a kind of reverse sexism? Isn't it also, she notes, the logic that has led so many women to take part in terrorist groups such as the Palestinian commandos, the Baader-Meinhoff Gang, and the Red Brigades?

A NEW GENERATION

But the more astute members of this and subsequent generations, Kristeva hopes, will do something else. First, they will avoid romanticizing "Woman." She repeats Lacan's "scandalous pronouncement" that "[t]here is no such thing as Woman." Indeed, she says, "she does not exist with a capital 'W,' as a holder of a mythical plenitude, a supreme power upon which the terror of power as well as terrorism as the desire for power base themselves" (1995: 218). The second generation's monolithic conception of Woman erased actual women's individuality and specificity. The task of the third generation will be to attend to the singularity of each woman. "The most subtle aspects of the new generation's feminist subversion will be directed toward this issue in the future," Kristeva writes. And then she outlines what she hopes will be a third generation's aim: "This focus will combine the sexual with the symbolic in order to discover first the specificity of the feminine and then the specificity of each woman" (ibid.: 210).

Second, Kristeva thinks the next generation will look for ways to reconcile women's multiple desires. The third generation will take seriously women's desire to have children alongside their desire to enter the male world of linear time – that is, to have children *and* have careers. None of the previous generations of women had a way for women to see themselves as both reproducers of the species and producers of culture, that is, as both of the body and of the social. The choice always seemed to be between the self-abnegating activity of mothering versus the self-affirming activity of culture. Now:

> if maternity is to be guilt-free, this journey needs to be undertaken without masochism and without annihilating one's affective, intellectual, and professional personality, either. In this way, maternity becomes a true *creative act*, something that we have not yet been able to imagine.
>
> (ibid.: 220)

Third, this new generation will be more effective in what the second generation began: analyzing the dynamics of signs in the psycho-symbolic structure. The second generation saw this structure and simply tried to reject it:

> For this third generation, which I strongly support (which I am imagining?), the dichotomy between man and women as an opposition between two rival entities is *a problem for metaphysics*. What does "identity" and even "sexual identity" mean in a theoretical and scientific space in which the notion of "identity" itself is challenged? I am not simply alluding to bisexuality, which most often reveals a desire for totality, a desire for the eradication of difference. I am thinking more specifically of subduing the "fight to the finish" between rival groups, not in hopes of reconciliation – since at the very least, feminism can be lauded for bringing to light that which is irreducible and even lethal in the social contract – but in the hopes that the violence occurs with the utmost mobility within individual and sexual identity, and not through a rejection of the other.
>
> (ibid.: 223)

The third generation will need to recognize that the psychosymbolic structure is based upon a metaphysics of identity and difference, where one sex (or class or race or nation) is seen as a rival of another.

But instead of shunning this structure, Kristeva calls on us to *internalize* it, to see within ourselves the "fundamental separation of the sociosymbolic contract" (ibid.: 223). "From that point on, the other is neither an evil being foreign to me nor a scapegoat from the outside, that is, of another sex, class, race, or nation," Kristeva writes. "I am *at once the attacker and the victim*, the same *and* the other, identical *and* foreign" (ibid.). This seems at first to be a truly scandalous "solution" – for how would internalizing the rivalries of the structure help transform the structure? Kristeva suggests that this process will first remind us that each person's "identity" patches together a diversity of ethnic, regional, sexual, professional, and political identifications. Second, the process will hold each person accountable: "I simply have to analyze incessantly the fundamental separation of my own untenable identity" (ibid.). We will realize that, insofar as we each have an identity (a sense of self) *thanks to* the sociosymbolic contract, we each are implicated in all its dirty deeds.

Raising the issues of responsibility and accountability at the end of the essay, Kristeva returns to the theme she discussed in "Stabat Mater": ethics or morality. She reiterates that women may not be subject to old, classical ethics, but may instead be able to point toward a new ethics. Unfortunately, Kristeva has precious little to say here about what she means. She suggests that two practices can open the field for this new ethics, psychoanalysis and aesthetics. These practices undermine the old anthropomorphic (i.e. male-shaped) identities of language and community. They will remind us of the "diversity of our identifications and the relativity of our symbolic and biological existence" (ibid.):

> Understood as such, aesthetics takes on the question of morality. The imaginary helps to outline an ethics that remains invisible, as the outbreak of the imposture and of hatred wreaks havoc on societies freed from dogmas and laws. As restriction and as play, the imaginary enables us to envision an ethics aware of its own sacrificial order and that thus retains part of the burden for each of its adherents, whom the imaginary pronounces guilty and responsible, though it offers them the direct possibility of jouissance, of various aesthetic productions, of having a life filled with trials and differences. This would be a utopian ethics, but is any other kind possible?

> (ibid.: 223–224)

In the end, Kristeva's discussion of a third generation of feminism is less about the gains that could be made for women and more about the gains that can be made for human beings. Instead of positioning "patriarchy" and men as the culprits who have oppressed women, it argues that all people are equally guilty – and equally capable of bringing about a new ethical vision. Rather than reinstate or revalue the previous hierarchies of male versus female, it calls on us to recognize the many rivalries we have within us. It calls on us to put our own house in order first.

SUMMARY

Kristeva's essay, "Women's Time," draws together themes present in "Stabat Mater," along with themes she later develops in her psychoanalytic works of the 1980s. A unifying theme is her focus on the sociosymbolic order. The first generation of feminists sought ways for women to join that order, but they did little to try to evaluate or change it. The second generation repudiated it, but in the process risked becoming just as sexist or even violent as the order it found so reprehensible. Kristeva holds out hope that a third generation of feminists will try to critically and productively re-evaluate this order, while urging women to take to heart their own culpability in it. At bottom, Kristeva's focus on the sociosymbolic order calls on men and women to rethink their most fundamental views about what it is to be masculine and feminine, how their identities are constructed, and how they cannot escape these constructions in search of some androgynous alternative. Kristeva likes sexual difference, but she wants this difference to be one that is neither masochistic nor constraining, but, rather, productive and freeing for women and their sexuality.

7

REVOLT

Through Julia Kristeva's theoretical framework, a particular conception of the person or "speaking being" emerges: one who is, on the
one hand, immersed in the logical order of symbolic meaning, where
identity (between, for example, a signifier and its signified) reigns; but
one who is, on the other hand, riven by the body's and the psyche's
semiotic charges and energy displacements. The speaking being is a
subject in process because her identity is never fixed in place; her identity is continuously disrupted by semiotic language's heterogeneity,
polyphony, and polysemy (that is, the many and varied sounds and
meanings produced by semiotic language). In Kristeva's view, the two
poles the speaking being, the semiotic and symbolic, are simultaneously at work. Even though the symbolic mode is usually more
prominent, it would be disastrous for either side to triumph altogether.
Someone who lacks any semiotic energy might as well be, perhaps must
already be, dead. Yet someone who is governed exclusively by semiotic charges is psychotic, thoroughly out of touch with meaning and
identity. The subject in process has to traverse a treacherous terrain,
energized by destabilizing biological and psychological charges, while
still able to negotiate competently in the symbolic. Even as semiotic
charges disrupt her attempts at being a self-identical, stable subject, she
must carry on as if she were one. In other words, speaking beings have
to keep the semiotic *chora* intact but at bay.

This project certainly calls for a great deal of effort on the part of borderline subjects, those who are already having difficulty maintaining a stable identity. Such subjects have a loose hold on the symbolic and their own sense of being a stable self. Their semiotic charges are in a constant state of revolt against symbolic order.

It might seem that those who have a firmer hold on the symbolic are in much better shape. But this is not necessarily the case. There is another peril awaiting those who have lost touch with the force of the semiotic. Without the threat of revolt against the symbolic order, the psyche loses energy. It loses the life-enhancing force that the *chora* brings to subjectivity. The self becomes more of an automaton than a human being. The less touch people have with semiotic forces, the less able they are to thrive, change, and live. Instead of being the kinds of open systems described in Chapter 2, in which people are open to psychic and somatic energy from within themselves and from those around them, people become closed off. Instead of being in love and alive, they are in isolation. No living being can thrive this way. There must always be an avenue by which the semiotic can revolt against symbolic order.

This chapter takes up Kristeva's conception of revolt in three ways: first, by surveying how contemporary society threatens to deaden the subject's psyche; second, by looking at the way that Kristeva thinks the subject can and should revolt against our psyche-numbing society; and, third, by assessing the extent to which Kristeva's conception of revolt is political. The chapter will show that, in the process of writing about revolt, Kristeva demonstrates how attending to the "micropolitics" of subject identity-formation is as necessary to political transformation as the "macropolitics" that occurs within the public sphere. From a Kristevan point of view, the public and the private should never be neatly separated.

THE SOCIETY OF THE SPECTACLE

Today's subjects, Kristeva finds, are more at risk of losing touch with the semiotic than of losing touch with the "reality" constituted through symbolic meaning – not so much because they are too immersed in the symbolic, but because they have become anesthetized to semiotic energy. We are so bombarded by the stimuli of empty images that we cease to feel or respond in any genuine way. Today's world is marked

THE ROOTS OF REVOLT

Kristeva approaches the concept of revolt in the broadest sense, first by looking at the etymology of the term. What now has a thoroughly political connotation began as a term referring to turning. As she writes:

> The Latin verb *volvere*, which is at the origin of "revolt," was initially far removed from politics. It produced derivatives with meanings – semes – such as "curve," "entourage," "turn," "return." In Old French, it can mean "to envelop," "curvature," "vault," and even "omelet," "to roll," and "to roll oneself in"; the extensions go as far as "to loaf about" (*galvauder*), "to repair," and "vaudeville" (*vaudevire*, "refrain").
>
> (2000: 1)

By the sixteenth century, the Italian emphasis on the circular movement of time creeps into the term, as do the conceptions of *volubility* and the concept of wrapping paper around a stick resulting in a *volume*:

> The linguist Alain Rey stresses the cohesion of these diverse etymological evolutions, which start with a matrix and driving idea: "to twist, roll, wrap" (going back to the Sanskrit *varutram*, the Greek *elutron*, *eiluma*) and "covering," an object that serves as a wrapping.
>
> (ibid.: 2)

In all these derivations, the topological and technical ideas of twisting or enveloping dominate, even appearing in the name of the Swedish automobile company, Volvo ("I roll"):

> The old Indo-European forms *wel* and *welu* evoke a voluntary, artisanal act, resulting in the denomination of technical objects that protect and envelop. Today we are barely aware of the intrinsic links between "revolution" and "helix," "to rebel" (*se révolter*), and "to wallow" (*se vautrer*).
>
> (ibid.)

Over time, then, revolt has meant a turning in time, space, and kind. The term itself is malleable and it has suggested different forms of social, political, and ethical transformation. Kristeva draws on all these meanings in her writings on revolt.

by the "society of the spectacle," Kristeva notes, drawing on the work
of the radical intellectual, Guy Debord (1931–1994), who was founder
and editor of the journal, *Internationale Situationniste*, from 1958 to 1969
and the author of *Society of the Spectacle* (1983), first published as
La société du spectacle in 1967.

In the first of the 221 aphorisms in *Society of the Spectacle*, Debord
notes that, in modern societies, "all of life presents itself as an immense
accumulation of *spectacles*. Everything that was directly lived has
moved away into a representation" (1983: no. 1). The spectacle is the
"concrete inversion of life" (ibid.: 2), "the unrealism of the real society"
(ibid.: 6), and has many forms – advertising, information, propaganda,
and entertainment – all of which are manifestations of the underlying
economic and productive order. Modern production, under both
capitalism and socialism, makes the commodity king. We live in a
world in which what we buy, wear, and consume defines us. And we
try to fulfill our thin but insatiable desires by consuming more and
more. "The spectacle subjugates living men to itself to the extent
that the economy has totally subjugated them. It is no more than the
economy developing for itself. It is the true reflection of the production of things, and the false objectification of the producers" (ibid.: 16).
In other words, in the society of the spectacle, people are tools of the
economy; their desires are not their own; desires are manufactured as
surely as are the commodities meant to fulfill them. We consume to
meet our needs, unaware that what we take to be a "need" has been
artificially produced. "To the extent that necessity is socially dreamed,
the dream becomes necessary. The spectacle is the nightmare of
imprisoned modern society which ultimately expresses nothing more
than its desire to sleep. The spectacle is the guardian of sleep" (ibid.:
20). In the society of the spectacle, people's desires are, ultimately,
aimed at oblivion. We consume, and therefore we need not have any
real aspirations of our own.

Though Kristeva only mentions Debord a few times in her work,
much of her writing is clearly influenced by him and offers parallel
assessments. Sometimes she uses his language of "the spectacle"; at
other times, she refers to the "culture of the show." Still, she is pointing
to the same phenomenon. Echoing Debord, Kristeva writes: "You are
overwhelmed with images. They carry you away, they replace you, you
are dreaming. The rapture of the hallucination originates in the absence
of boundaries between pleasure and reality, between truth and false-

hood. The spectacle is life as a dream – we all want this" (1995: 8). With Debord, Kristeva points to the way the society of the spectacle inverts reality – instead of experiencing the shallowness and meaninglessness of capitalist society, subjects begin to experience images as real. While Debord focuses on the way this phenomenon alters objective reality, Kristeva focuses on how it distorts subjective space.

In her book, *New Maladies of the Soul*, which she had written in 1993, Kristeva observes that a new kind of patient is appearing on psychoanalysts' couches. Today's patients seem to suffer from a withering of psychic space; they seem to have less of a "soul":

> Modern man is a narcissist – a narcissist who may suffer, but who feels no remorse. He manifests his suffering in his body and he is afflicted with somatic symptoms. His problems serve to justify his refuge in the very problems that his own desire paradoxically solicits. When he is not depressed, he becomes swept away by insignificant and valueless objects that offer a perverse pleasure, but no satisfaction. Living in a piecemeal and accelerated space and time, he often has trouble acknowledging his own physiognomy; left without a sexual, subjective, or moral identity, this amphibian is a being of boundaries, a borderline, or a "false self" – a body that acts, often without even the joys of such performative drunkenness. Modern man is losing his soul, but he does not know it, for the psychic apparatus is what registers representations and their meaningful values for the subject. Unfortunately, that darkroom needs repair.
>
> (Kristeva 1995: 8–9)

This is a powerful diagnosis of human beings' condition today: we are losing our souls – not in the Christian sense of the term, but in the sense that we no longer have an "inner garden," a place to keep alive, nurture, and tend a meaning of our existence. Later in *New Maladies of the Soul*, she describes the alternatives in this way:

> I am picturing a sprawling metropolis with glass and steel buildings that reach to the sky, reflect it, reflect each other, and reflect you – a city filled with people steeped in their own image who rush about with overdone make-up on and who are cloaked in gold, pearls, and fine leather, while in the next street over, heaps of filth abound and drugs accompany the sleep or the fury of the social outcasts.
>
> This city could be New York; it could be any future metropolis, even your own.

What might one do in such a city? Nothing but buy and sell goods and images, which amounts to the same thing, since they both are dull, shallow symbols. Those who can or wish to preserve a lifestyle that downplays opulence as well as misery will need to create a space for an "inner zone" – a secret garden, an intimate quarter, or more simply and ambitiously, a psychic life.

(ibid.: 27)

Before she addresses how this secret garden could be created, Kristeva has more to say about the problem of living in the society of the spectacle. Suffering, but often unaware that they are, modern individuals reach for a remedy in a bottle of pills or liquor, addressing the collapse of psychic space with a tonic for the body. "The body conquers the invisible territory of the soul" (ibid.: 9). Kristeva laments the contemporary loss of psychic space and the concomitant impetus to anesthetize this loss with drugs and alcohol. And she notices another kind of anesthetic at work today, which Debord had seen as well. (Debord committed suicide a year after *New Maladies of the Soul* was originally published.) The premier anesthetic in the society of the spectacle is the spectacle itself, primarily in the form of the mass media:

If drugs do not take over your life, your wounds are "healed" with images, and before you can speak about your states of the soul, you drown them in the world of mass media. The image has an extraordinary power to harness your anxieties and desires, to take on their intensity and to suspend their meaning. It works by itself.

(ibid.: 8)

Note that there is a very odd logic in society-as-anesthetic: it fulfills desires while simultaneously stripping the subject's capacity to desire. Ultimately, the process of seeking satisfaction in the society of the spectacle alienates the subject from herself. Silently drawing on the work of the German philosopher and revolutionary, Karl Marx (1818–1883), Debord identified how this logic manifested itself economically: in their capacities as workers or producers, people produce the means of their own alienation. Debord writes:

The worker does not produce himself . . . he produces an independent power. The success of this production, its abundance, returns to the producer as an *abundance of dispossession*. All the time and space of his world become *foreign* to him with the accumulation of his alienated products. The spectacle is the map of this new world, a map which exactly covers its territory.

(1983: 31)

Kristeva focuses on the psychological manifestations of this logic. Immersion in the society of the spectacle blocks, inhibits, and even destroys psychic life (Kristeva 1995: 8). This process is creating a new kind of patient who arrives in the psychoanalyst's office with traditional symptoms, but whose "'maladies of the soul' soon break through their hysterical and obsessional allure – 'maladies of the soul' that are not necessarily psychoses, but that evoke the psychotic patient's inability to symbolize his unbearable traumas" (ibid.: 9). Whatever their true diagnoses, all their symptoms "share a common denominator – the inability to represent" (ibid.). Accordingly, Kristeva notes two kinds of alienation that occur. One occurs among depressives who become alienated from their own words. They speak as if they were automatons.

The other alienation occurs at the level of the relationship of oneself to one's body. As she says in her more recent book, *The Sense and Non-sense of Revolt* (published in French in 1996 and in English in 2000), in the new economic order:

it is worth looking at what is becoming of the individual. . . . Consider the status of the individual in the face of biological technologies. The human being tends to disappear as a person with rights, since he/she is negotiated as possessing organs that are convertible into cash. We are exiting the era of the subject and entering that of the patrimonial individual.

(2000: 6)

Kristeva uses this odd phrase, "patrimonial individual" (or, in the original, *personne patrimoniale*), to connote an individual who is so alienated from herself that she considers her body an inheritance (patrimony) that she might dispose of like any other inheritance:

"I" am not a subject, as psychoanalysis continues to assert, attempting the rescue – indeed the salvation – of subjectivity; "I" am not a transcendental subject either, as classical philosophy would have it. Instead, "I" am, quite simply, the owner of my genetic or organo-physiological patrimony; "I" possess my organs, and that only in the best-case scenario, for there are countries where organs are stolen in order to be sold. The whole question is whether my patrimony should be remunerated or free: whether "I" can enrich myself or, as an altruist, forgo payment in the name of humanity or whether "I," as a victim, am dispossessed of it.

(ibid.)

Alienated from her own body, anesthetized by the spectacles of contemporary society, the modern subject is cut off from any meaningful psychic life. She is losing her soul. And so she is in dire need of a revolt against the deadening symbolic order of modern life. For these reasons, Kristeva has spent much of her life calling for a revolution – not so much a political one as a cultural and psychological one. Ultimately, Kristeva believes, such revolutions are the only ones that might have any lasting political effects.

THE CULTURE AND NECESSITY OF REVOLT

At the beginning of *The Sense and Non-sense of Revolt*, Kristeva reminds the reader of Europe's tradition of revolt:

Europeans are cultured in the sense that culture is their critical conscience; it suffices to think of Cartesian doubt, the freethinking of the Enlightenment, Hegelian negativity, Marx's thought, Freud's unconscious, not to mention Zola's *J'accuse* and formal revolts such as Bauhaus and surrealism, Artaud and Stockhausen, Picasso, Pollock, and Francis Bacon. The great moments of twentieth-century art and culture are moments of formal and metaphysical revolt.

(2000: 6–7)

The twentieth century also saw some of the worst times for revolt, especially under the reign of the notorious Soviet leader, Joseph Stalin (1879–1953), during which revolt deviated into "terror and bureaucracy" (ibid.: 7).

This culture of revolt is now in danger of extinction. It is caught between two impasses: "the failure of rebellious ideologies, on the one hand, and the surge of consumer culture, on the other" (ibid.). An incessant concern of Kristeva's, throughout her writing career, has been the need for revolt. In her book of 1974, translated as *Revolution in Poetic Language*, Kristeva considers the ways in which avant-garde poets revolt against the fixed meaning of symbolic discourse. She considers the revolutionary potential of semiotically charged language. Instead of treating literary texts as dead relics ("a mere depository of thin linguistic layers, an archive of structures"), she thinks of the ways they offer "productive violence" (1984: 16). In her hands, "the text is a practice that could be compared to political revolution: the one brings about in the subject what the other introduces into society" – that is, a transformation. Revolt is a "structuring and de-structuring *practice*, a passage to the outer *boundaries* of the subject and society. Then – and only then – can it be jouissance and revolution" (ibid.: 17).

Revolt is necessary for the psyche and society. In *The Sense and Nonsense of Revolt*, she argues that we should not allow the culture of the show to supplant the culture of revolt. As psychoanalysis shows:

> Happiness exists only at the price of a revolt. None of us has pleasure without confronting an obstacle, prohibition, authority, or law that allows us to realize ourselves as autonomous and free. The revolt revealed to accompany the private experience of happiness is an integral part of the pleasure principle. Furthermore, on the social level, the normalizing order is far from perfect and fails to support the excluded: jobless youth, the poor in the projects, the homeless, the unemployed, and foreigners, among many others. When the excluded have no culture of revolt and must content themselves with ideologies, with shows and entertainments that far from satisfy the demand of pleasure, they become rioters.
>
> (Kristeva 2000: 7)

So, given the stranglehold that bureaucracy, terror, and the culture of the show have put on revolt, what kind of revolt can be had today? She begins each of three of her more recent works with this question: "What revolt today?" (*Quelle révolte aujourd'hui?*). She asks the question in the mid-1990s at the start of the first volume of her series on the powers and limits of psychoanalysis, *The Sense and Non-sense of Revolt*, then again in 1996 in the second volume of the series, *La révolte intime* (*Intimate Revolt*), and once more in 1997 at the start of her short book, *L'avenir d'une révolte* (*The Future of Revolt*). With each posing of the question, she takes up a different angle. *The Sense and Non-sense of Revolt* focuses on the necessity of revolt for developing and maintaining a psychic life. The 1996 book, *La révolte intime*, explores the necessity of revolt for the experience of intimacy. And her 1997 volume, *L'avenir d'une révolte*, considers revolt in terms of experiences of liberty in psychoanalysis and literature.

What revolt today? In an era when anything new, novel, or disruptive is immediately co-opted into the same, this really is a pressing question. What revolt can there be in a world in which, as Kristeva puts the question, the culture of the show has supplanted the culture of revolt?

SO YOU WANT TO HAVE A REVOLUTION?

As mentioned above, Kristeva's early work on revolt attended to the revolutionary potential of avant-garde literature. But, by the 1990s, she saw the limits of this approach, namely, that textual analysis had become something of a dogma in the best universities in France and the United States, and that it was time to attend to experience, which she says "includes the pleasure principle as well as the rebirth of meaning for the other" (2000: 8). Her main point of departure is Freud's theory and what it has to say about psychoanalytic as well as aesthetic experience.

Freud identified two kinds of revolt: Oedipal revolt and the return to the archaic. The first kind, Oedipal revolt, can be seen as a way the psyche is structured: "the Oedipus complex and the incest taboo organize the psyche of the speaking being" (ibid.: 12). In other words, the mind or personality of each individual develops in response to his or her desire for his or her mother – and the taboo that censors this desire. Oedipal revolt can also be seen historically, at least in Freud's historical account of how civilization arose as a revolt against patriarchal authority. In his book, *Totem and Taboo*, Freud tells an apocryphal story of a primitive society in which a leader and father figure kept all the women to himself. The sons killed the father so that they could have access to these women as well; but forever after – including all subsequent generations – they were overcome with guilt and so set up rituals of penance, self-denial, and sacrifice to compensate for their crime. As Kristeva summarizes: "Freud attributes the origin of civilization to nothing less than the murder of the father, which means that the transmission and permanence of the oedipal over generations can be understood in light of a phylogenetic hypothesis" (ibid.). Each generation, as well as each individual, replays the Oedipal revolt when it imagines patricide as a way to maintain access to the maternal body. But the result is guilt and the incest taboo, something of a dead end for revolution. "Hasn't this logic," Kristeva asks, "which Freud brought to the fore and which characterizes the religious, social, and artistic man, reached a saturation point? Perhaps this is where we are: neither guilty nor responsible but consequently incapable of revolt" (ibid.: 15).

Kristeva locates Freud's second kind of revolt, the return to the archaic, through a letter Freud wrote in 1936 to the Swiss philosopher and psychoanalyst, Ludwig Binswanger (1881–1966):

> Objecting to Binswanger's philosophical flights and metaphysical specula-tions, which he finds far removed from both the clinic and the scientific thought he considers to be his own, Freud writes: "I have always dwelt only in the ground floor and basement of the building. . . . In that you are the conser-vative, I am the revolutionary. Had I only another life of work before me I should dare to offer even those highly born people a home in my lowly dwelling." (Translation: you are highly placed; I would like to offer people like you who deign to accord me some attention a place in this basement where I am trying to develop a revolutionary spirit.)
>
> (ibid.)

Kristeva sees a "juncture between this image of the 'lowly,' 'revo-lutionary' house and the series of archaeological metaphors in Freud whereby the unconscious is presented as invisible, hidden away, low." She argues that Freud's use of the word *revolutionary* "has nothing to do with moral, much less political, revolt." It signifies instead "the possi-bility that psychoanalysis has to access the archaic, to overturn conscious meaning" (ibid.). Freud's revolutionary work is in search of "the impossible temporality that is timelessness (the unconscious has been unaware of time since [Freud's book of 1900] *The Interpretation of Dreams*)" (ibid.: 15–16). In Kristeva's estimation, "Freud is a revolu-tionary in search of lost time" (ibid.: 16). For example, Freud's notion of the uncanny (or *das Unheimliche*) points to experiences that shake our own temporal foundations and allow us access to time lost or forgotten in the normalizing order. Kristeva explores how this kind of revolt is at work in aesthetic and analytic experience:

> The return, or access, to the archaic as access to a timeless temporality . . . prepares us for benevolence. Isn't a good analyst one who welcomes us with

benevolence, with indulgence, without scores to settle, calmly, in a lowly dwelling, as Freud says, and this sense, a revolutionary one, giving us access to our own "lowly dwelling"?

(ibid.)

These two kinds of revolt found in the analytic experience suggest, Kristeva says (ibid.), three figures of revolt:

- revolt as the transgression of a prohibition;
- revolt as repetition, working-through, working-out; and
- revolt as displacement, combinatives, games.

Kristeva uses these themes, which occupy much of her writings on revolt, to analyze three twentieth-century writers: the existentialist, Jean-Paul Sartre (1905–1980), the surrealist poet, Louis Aragon (1897–1982), and the theorist mentioned in this book's introduction, Roland Barthes. These writers are exemplars of a rebel culture, of a culture of revolt that is in danger of extinction, but still possible if we pursue it.

All three writers share a focus in their revolutionary texts: "a revolt against identity: the identity of sex and meaning, of ideas and politics, of being and the other" (ibid.: 18). For example, Kristeva sees a rebel in Barthes, despite his "elegant and reserved persona," because of the way he sought to undo and displace the meaning of texts (including the "text" of fashion) that others considered natural (ibid.: 188–189). Barthes took issue with any supposed naturalness of meaning. He even questioned "the possibility of meaning itself" as well as the unity of any interpreter. He asked, Kristeva writes: "Is there a unity – an 'I,' a 'we' – that can have meaning or seek meaning?" (ibid.: 189). Barthes' revolt was againt the unity of any meaning, either by way of the product or the producer.

Such a revolt – whether that of Barthes or of any of the other writers she considers – could not and should not win out entirely, for that would spell the end of any possibility of being a coherent, speaking being. Speaking beings have a psychological and biological need to maintain their identity. But at the same time they must loosen "the structures concerning 'one's own' and the 'identical,' 'true' and 'false,' 'good' and 'bad'" lest they die, because "symbolic organizations, like organisms, endure on the condition of renewal and joy" (ibid.: 18).

Kristeva sees promise in Aragon, Sartre, and Barthes, because their "revolt against the One" suggests:

> another structuring of subjectivity. Another humanity, we might say peremp-
> torily, can be heard not only in their thought but also – and this is essential,
> for it signals the depth of the phenomenon – in their language: a humanity that
> takes the risk of confronting religion and the metaphysics that nourishes it,
> confronting the meaning of language.

> (ibid.)

So, Kristeva holds out hope for nothing less than a new humanity, one in which each individual can express her specificity while still being a part of her tribe. Each person will be able to assert her uniqueness by pushing the limits of the language that her tribe hands her. Kristeva is pointing toward a way out of the quagmire of choices the contemporary era has handed us: where one either argues for universal human rights or distinct identity differences. "Repressive returns to systems foregrounding the needs of identity are resurfacing: nationalism, traditionalism, conservatism, fundamentalism, and so on. Thought is content to build archives: we take stock and kneel down before the relics of the past in a museumlike culture or, in the case of popular variants, in a culture of distraction" (ibid.: 19). Kristeva thinks there is still the chance for something more, a human life in which revolt can keep alive "the capacity for enthusiasm, doubt, and the pleasure of inquiry" (ibid.).

After all this talk of revolution, the reader might wonder: How political are Kristeva's ideas about revolt? Kelly Oliver faults Kristeva for her turn away from politics, noting "Kristeva's aestheticization of poetic revolution in *Powers of Horror*." Oliver writes:

> whereas in her earlier work Kristeva describes the revolution in poetic
> language as a political revolution, in *Powers of Horror* it becomes a purely
> aesthetic revolution. While there may be a relation between aesthetic experi-
> ence and political revolution, Kristeva does not make that relation explicit in
> her text.

> (1993: 10–11)

By the mid-1970s, Kristeva had turned away from politics on the large scale and toward politics at the level of the individual, drawing especially on her vocation as a psychoanalyst. In several interviews, Kristeva has discussed her move away from trying to address politics on the macro scale to her work at the psychoanalytic, small scale. "I don't think we can approach political questions with a general discourse," she says (Guberman 1996: 24). "It would be better to take up again the basic presuppositions, start from the small things, the small notions" (ibid.: 15). Rather than take up the grand problems of history, she prefers to look at "the minimal components that constitute the speaking being" (ibid.). The "concrete problems" that she has concerned herself with, since her refusal of Maoism, are love, melancholia, and abjection. She sees these as political as well as personal problems. She notes: "I consider that my work as an analyst is political work, to take it in a microscopic and individual sense" (ibid.: 42).

In her more recent writings on revolt, Kristeva does distinguish psychological revolt from societal revolt. Though the two are distinct, she seems to think both are vitally important. But, unlike most theorists of political revolution, Kristeva points to the fundamental necessity of psychological revolt – revolt against identity, homogenization, the spectacle, and the law. If we do not keep alive an inner zone, a secret garden, a life of the mind, Kristeva suggests, there is little possibility for any meaningful political revolt. Unless the individual keeps her own specificity and soul alive, any other revolution will lead to bureaucratization and terror. Such, at least, is the lesson of many of the "revolutions" of the twentieth century – and the more recent nationalist and ethnic uprisings of our own day.

SUMMARY

In her writings on revolt, Kristeva shows the need for a culture of revolt. Without revolt, the human psyche is in danger of atrophying and withering away. To create and maintain a psychic space or inner zone, speaking beings need to revolt against the culture of the show, against rigid symbolic structures, and against homogeneous identities. Drawing on aesthetic and analytic experience, Kristeva shows how speaking beings can keep alive the possibility of renewal and revolt.

AFTER KRISTEVA

Kristeva occasionally likens herself to being a stranger, a foreigner speaking something other than her native tongue, Bulgarian, living in a country where she will always be deemed as the other. Though she began learning French before she was five years old, her Eastern European visage and accent betrays that she is not a part of "the same" and as a consequence she, like any foreigner, can seem to be a threat to identity and order. She describes herself as someone who disturbs or unsettles the status quo, as the vigilant outsider. This plays out, in part, in the difficulty of her texts. They are known for being daunting and demanding texts to read, for even the more educated of readers. As a result, her name may be known much more than the subtleties of her theory. This has, I think, set an odd limit to her influence.

The limit is not one of scope: her work has been used in philosophy, psychology, feminist theory, art criticism, cultural studies, and, especially, literary theory. The limit is really one of – dare I say – penetration. Within any given field, Kristeva's approach is one of several from which one might draw, but it does not seem to have necessarily any more of a hold than any other. If one's aim in doing theory is to be *au courant*, one might get away without struggling with Julia Kristeva. There are plenty of other approaches with a much flatter learning curve.

But if one aims to do something else – namely, to look at the intersection of what we call "culture" and "nature" in any given area of human endeavor – then reading Kristeva will pay off immensely. Theorists from across the fields have drawn on Kristeva's work to look into how the speaking, desiring, subject in process influences art, literature, dance, philosophy, and theology.

BODIES, TEXTS, AND WOMEN

Kristeva's work has probably had the greatest impact in literary theory and feminist thought. Many literary critics have engaged Kristeva's notion that the literary text can never be taken again as signifying univocally, without any semiotic disruptions or with any fixed meaning. As a creation of dynamic, speaking beings, literary texts portend a disruption – and yet also a renewal – of the subjectivity of both writers and readers. Many literary critics in Canada, the United States, England, Australia, and New Zealand, to mention just the English-speaking world, work on Kristeva, including Judith Butler, Marilyn Edelstein, Alice Jardine, Lisa Lowe, Tilottama Rajan, Frances Restuccia, Jacqueline Rose, and Ewa Ziarek. For example, a scholar of English literature, Anna Smith of New Zealand, has written a volume on Kristeva's application in literary theory, especially regarding the disturbing effect that literature can have on its readers (Smith 1996). Kristeva's work is a regular feature in courses in literary theory and it is included in anthologies used in comparative literature seminars, including the volume, *Critical Theory Since 1965*, edited by Hazard Adams and Leroy Searle. On a regular basis at the American Modern Language Association meetings, panels are devoted to Kristeva's work. She has also been an invited speaker at conferences in literary theory, including the International Association of Philosophy and Literature. As one might imagine, Kristeva's work has also influenced scholars who work on French literature, including Joan Brandt and Suzanne Guerlac.

Turning to another field of experience, Chapters 5 and 6 of this book showed how Kristeva's work has shaken up feminist theory, sometimes by turning sacred distinctions on their heads. Kristeva refuses to respect, for example, a distinction between sex and gender, arguing that what these terms respectively represent – biology and culture – cannot be neatly demarcated. They are always imbricated and intermeshed in our daily, lived experience. Accordingly, Kristeva gives credence to the salience of biological, sexual difference. There is a relevant dimension of somatic and energized bodily experience that comes with being a particular sexual being. But this dimension is not purely biological, for our somatic experience can only be made sense of when it enters culture, that is, when we begin to interpret and speak. Kristeva's French, post-structuralist treatment of biology and culture is much more subtle and nuanced than many Anglo-American feminist accounts, thus offering ample opportunities for misreading her work. I discussed one of these misreadings in Chapter 5: the notion that Kristeva is an essentialist.

In an interview with Ross Guberman, Kristeva addresses the gulf between French and American notions of difference and universalism. The American experience, politically speaking, has been to "establish the separation of the sexes: women are clearly set aside because of their 'difference,' but this difference is limited to sensibility or motherhood and does not strive for shared social participation" (Guberman 1996: 268). Women in France, conversely, have been included as part of the voice of the nation, allowing them to help articulate the public opinion that might challenge the political authority of the sovereign. But, in this respect, French women have gained universality at the expense of their particularity. The reactions to these experiences have been varied in both countries. But, perhaps, the reason that American feminists are so sensitive to anything that resembles essentialism is that, in their experience, women were denied political autonomy due to their "essential" differences. So, talking about biology is always risky. Yet Kristeva tries to clarify why this risk is important:

Thinking about the feminine, but also about other cultural experiences of difference (such as poetic language and contemporary art and poetry, which are in no way mere "deviations" from the norm) led me to articulate my notion of the semiotic and symbolic. For every speaking being, the symbolic is the horizon of the "universal" bond with other members of his group and is rooted in the signs and syntax of his national language. The semiotic is transverbal: it is made up of archaic representatives of drives and the senses that depend on the mother and biology. Both men and women, in different ways according to their psychic structures and their histories, combine these components to become "different" and "universal," singular and compatible.

(ibid.: 268–269)

Insofar as we all – men and women – are born of mothers, we are each privy to the *chora* and will signify semiotically as well as symbolically. Kristeva takes exception to those who have characterized the semiotic as a female essence. This is reductive, she says. "My goal is to inscribe difference at the heart of the universal and to contribute to what is much more difficult than war: the possibility, with a little bit of luck, that men and women, two human species with sometimes conflicting desires, will find a way to understand each other" (ibid.: 269).

KRISTEVA AND THE POLITICAL

As a political philosopher, I first turned to Kristeva because I was looking for an honest account of what it is to be a human being, a state I knew did not coincide with the Enlightenment account of an individual who knows well his own mind. I knew myself and others to be riven with impulses, desires, energy, conflict, and hidden abysses. I was looking for an account of human experience and agency in all its complexity, without any rosy glasses, that I could then use to try to assess whether human beings could be democratic political actors. Kristeva's view of subjectivity, for all its complexity and theoretical abstraction, struck me as really quite *true*: as speaking beings we are the subjects of and subject to semiotic and symbolic processes; we are open systems made and remade through our relationships with others; our aesthetic and literary creations are also, concomitantly, ways we create and recreate ourselves; our affects are as important as our intellect; and we are embodied beings subject to the vicissitudes of desire, not always in control of our destinations. Others have rejected Kristeva's account of being human precisely on these grounds. They have said, in public and in private, that, if Kristeva's account is right, then democratic life could not be possible. In order to hold onto their hopes, such critics have said "no" to Kristeva.

In one of the first English-language assessments of Kristeva's work, the literary critic, Toril Moi, gives a clear and fair assessment of Kristeva's work. But, in closing her assessment, Moi reprimands Kristeva for what Moi takes to be a failure politically in the theory:

> One of the problems with [Kristeva's] account of the "revolutionary" subject is that it slides over the question of revolutionary agency. Who or what is acting

in Kristeva's subversive schemes? In a political context her emphasis on the semiotic as an unconscious force precludes any analysis of the conscious decision-making processes that must be part of any *collective* revolutionary project. The stress on negativity and disruption, rather than on questions of organization and solidarity, leads Kristeva in effect to an anarchist and subjectivist political position. And on this point I would agree with the Marxist-Feminist Literature Collective who arraign her poetics as "politically unsatisfactory." Allon White also accuses Kristeva of political ineffectiveness, claiming that her politics "remain purified anarchism in a perpetual state of self-dispersal."

(1985: 170)

There are two criticisms packed into this passage: (1) a rather uninteresting socialist criticism that Kristeva is not a socialist; and (2) a more interesting criticism that the Kristevan subject could not be completely cognizant of her own interests and aims. If the semiotic is an unconscious force, then the agent is not fully conscious! "In the end," Moi writes, "Kristeva is unable to account for the relations between the subject and society" (ibid.: 171).

For another example, one of Kristeva's most trenchant critics, whom I discussed in Chapter 5, the philosopher Nancy Fraser, writes that "neither half of Kristeva's split subject can be a feminist political agent." She goes onto say:

Nor, I submit, can the two halves be joined together. They tend rather simply to cancel one another out, one forever shattering the identitarian pretensions of the other, the second forever recuperating the first and reconstituting itself as before. The upshot is a paralyzing oscillation between identity and nonidentity without any determinate practical issue.

(1992: 189)

Fraser sees Kristeva's theory of the subject in process as counterproductive to political agency, both individually and collectively. Fraser argues that, for this reason, feminists should have only "minimal truck" with Kristeva.

In separate works, both the literary critic, Ewa Ziarek, and I have responded to Fraser's critique, claiming in effect that saying "no" to Kristeva's implicit political theory is mistaken. Rather, Kristeva's theory is politically promising because it calls on subjects to rethink

their own identity and in the process make possible a more concilia-
tory and open relationship with others. (See McAfee (1993), McAfee
(2000b), Ziarek (1995), and Ziarek (2001).) Along these lines,
other political theorists writing on nationalism and xenophobia have
drawn considerably on Kristeva's work on abjection. (See, for
example, Norma Claire Moruzzi's essay in Oliver (1993) and Moruzzi
(2000).)

Given that Moi was writing early in Kristeva's career, her criticism
is somewhat understandable. But, as this book has surveyed, Kristeva's
work of the past twenty years has covered much social ground, from
her concern with the new maladies of the soul spawned by a materi-
alist society to the flattening of the psyche in the society of the
spectacle. Even in the texts Moi analyzed, though, one can see that
Kristeva is thoroughly concerned with "the relations between the
subject and society." What is her theory of the speaking subject if not
an analysis of the way speaking beings negotiate and make sense of/in
their world? The socialist criticism, which Fraser also drew on as
discussed in Chapter 5, ultimately rests on the difficulty it finds with
any theory that does not give a straightforward account of how people
can collectively change the world. It rejects theories that address how
subjects might be less than certain of their own intentions, especially if
such theories suggest that this is part of the human condition. (Note
that Moi does not reject Kristeva out of hand; she offers her criticisms
as caveats only.)

If we appreciate Kristeva's project as one that tries to shed light on
how culture and nature (or thought and sexuality, as she sometimes
terms this duality) are always intertwined, we can see her writing as a
way to show that the subject is always acting in a social field, and thus
is always "being political" to a certain extent. Nonetheless, Kristeva has
had an ambivalent relationship with politics. As I mentioned in the
introduction to this book, "Why Kristeva?," she parted company
with politics "at the macro level" after her trip to China in 1974.
Subsequently, she has said, she turned to the politics of the micro level,
of the individual, primarily through the lens of psychoanalysis. And it
is worth pointing out that psychoanalysis is in the main an enterprise
geared toward the individual. But, as we have seen, Kristeva's individuals are always in a social field, in open systems, and, in good times,
in loving relationships. So, as a practicing psychoanalyst, Kristeva might
be considered a micro-political activist.

Despite her disavowal of macro politics, some of her writing has taken her there, notably in her texts, *Strangers to Ourselves* (1991) and *Nations without Nationalism* (1993). *Strangers to Ourselves* visits a problem that Kristeva knows first-hand: the problem of being a foreigner and the difficulties that people and nations have with treating the foreigners in their midst. Kristeva's assessment of the problem draws on her grounding in psychoanalytic theory. We have difficulty welcoming strangers because of the difficulty we have accepting the stranger within, the unconscious. If we can come to terms with this stranger within then we might come to welcome those around us.

KRISTEVA, PHILOSOPHY, AND CULTURE

As a philosopher myself, I tend to think of Kristeva as a philosopher who has gone into the domains of literature and psychoanalysis. The truth is that she began as a student of the *nouveau roman*, but with a keen interest in the dynamics of meaning, a domain to which literary theorists, philosophers, linguists, semioticians, and cultural critics all lay claim. Kristeva's influence in philosophy has been pervasive, at least when one is thinking of the area of philosophy widely known as continental philosophy, as distinguished from the more dominant philosophical approach known as analytic or Anglo-American philosophy. In this latter field, Kristeva's influence is nearly non-existent, except for those feminist philosophers who are familiar with "the French feminists" and those analytic philosophers who may have an office down the hall from a continental philosopher.

But the effect that Kristeva has had in continental philosophy is substantial. Any continental philosopher should be at least minimally familiar with Kristeva's key ideas, especially the concepts of the semiotic and the symbolic, as well as her notions of abjection and the subject in process. And a good proportion of continental philosophers draw on her work extensively. For example, in the United States, Kelly Oliver began the early part of her impressive career focusing primarily on Kristeva (Oliver 1993a) and, more recently, she has used Kristeva's thought in her own books on Nietzsche, feminist thought, ethics, the family, and theories of recognition. Also, for example, Patricia Huntington has used Kristeva's thought as a point of departure for developing a political consciousness that is open to others (Huntington 1998); Allison Weir has used Kristeva to develop a theory of social identity (Weir 1996); and Sara Beardsworth is completing a book manuscript titled *Kristeva's Psycho-analytic, a Philosophy of Modernity*.

In the domains of cultural and aesthetic theory, philosophers, film studies scholars, and at least one sociologist (John Lechte) have taken Kristeva's work as a way to make sense of cinema and art. Prominent figures in film studies and aesthetics also include Tina Chanter, Hal Foster, Rosalind Krauss, and Kaja Silverman.

Kristeva's analysis of the Christian representation of the Virgin Mary, as well as her interpretations of religious history, have made their way into religious studies and theology. Leading figures in this field who draw on Kristeva include David Crownfield, David Fisher, Jean Graybeal, Diane Jonte-Pace, Cleo Kearns, and Martha Reineke. (For examples of their work, see Crownfield 1992.)

Julia Kristeva is very much a writer in process. In the last few years alone she has had two series of books come out in English and has written new ones that are still untranslated. So, it really is premature to write a chapter, much less to conclude one, titled "After Kristeva." It is better to look ahead, at her project – one that ought never to be completed; ultimately a transformation of the human race. Kristeva is, in the end, an optimist. As she said in an interview in 1996: "I feel as if a new humanity were being instituted – or unearthed. I'm speaking of another language, another mentality, another being – a genuine 'revolution' in mentalities" (Guberman 1996: 261).

FURTHER READING

WORKS BY JULIA KRISTEVA

FICTION

—— (1990) *Les Samouraïs*. Paris: Librairie Arthème Fayard. (English version, 1992, *The Samurai*, trans. Barbara Bray, New York: Columbia University Press.)

Like *The Mandarins*, a novel written by the early French feminist thinker, Simone de Beauvoir, this is a thinly veiled historical/fictional tale of the lives of the author's crowd from the Left Bank, including figures recognizably based on Lacan, Derrida, Barthes, and others.

—— (1991) *Le vieil homme et les loups*. Paris: Librairie Arthème Fayard. (English version, 1994, *The Old Man and the Wolves*, trans. Barbara Bray, New York: Columbia University Press.)

A radical departure from her other writings, *The Old Man and the Wolves* is a detective novel as well as a philosophical fable. In it, the protagonist, who is in mourning over her father's death, investigates the death of a Latin professor who was looking into disappearances involving wolves. This novel might be of interest to students and scholars wanting to explore the role of "the imaginary father" that Kristeva has invoked in her theoretical writings.

—— (1996) *Possessions*. Paris: Librairie Arthème Fayard. (English version, 1998, *Possessions*, trans. Barbara Bray, New York: Columbia University Press.)

With this novel, Kristeva continues her foray into the detective novel-cum-philosophical fable. Set in the same city and featuring the same protagonist as *The Old Man and the Wolves*, *Possessions* is a murder mystery investigating a woman's grisly decapitation.

THEORY

—— (1969) *Semiotiké: Recherches pour une sémanalyse*. Paris: Éditions du Seuil.

This was Kristeva's first book, a collection of essays published in a series from the journal *Tel Quel*. It has never been translated in its entirety into English, though two of its essays were translated and published in *Desire in Language*.

—— (1974) *La révolution du langage poétique*. Paris: Éditions du Seuil. (English version, 1984, *Revolution in Poetic Language*, trans. Leon S. Roudiez, New York: Columbia University Press.)

Kristeva presented this doctoral dissertation in 1973 and it is still, perhaps, her most important work. The French text includes her analysis of recent avant-garde writers. The English version contains only the theoretical parts of the book. In this she introduces her concepts of the *chora*, the semiotic and symbolic modes of signifiance, and begins her inquiry into the speaking subject. Unfortunately, the book may be the most difficult to read of all her works. It's still worth the effort, even if only to read (in the English version) part 1 and chapters 1 and 7 of part 2.

—— (1980) *Desire in Language*, trans. Thomas Gora, Alice Jardine, and Leon S. Roudiez and ed. by Leon S. Roudiez. New York: Columbia University Press.

This book is a collection of essays brought together by one of Kristeva's early translators, Leon S. Roudiez. In this volume, the reader can find some of Kristeva's earliest writings, including the marvelous essay, "Motherhood According to Bellini," complete with reproductions of the artist Bellini's portrayals of an antagonistic relationship between the Madonna and baby Jesus. Also, the volume includes the essay, "The Ethics of Linguistics," which is well worth reading.

—— (1980) *Pouvoirs de l'horreur*. Paris: Éditions du Seuil. (English version, 1982, *Powers of Horror: An Essay on Abjection*, trans. Leon S. Roudiez, New York: Columbia University Press.)

After nearly a decade of writing very dense and abstruse academese, Kristeva began writing in a new, more poetic and open style. This was her first book-length excursion into this kind of writing – and it makes for a very good read. The subject matter of the book is the process of abjection, the process by which a child who is still in the imaginary realm begins to expel from itself (physically and psychically) what it decides is not part of its own clean and proper self. This is the way the child begins to develop a sense of a discrete "I," rather than remaining part of an undifferentiated semiotic *chora*. Abjection begins in early childhood and it continues throughout one's life. What is abject is never excluded once and for all; it remains on the periphery of consciousness, haunting the ever-tenuous borders of selfhood. After developing her ideas about abjection, Kristeva applies them to the avant-garde writer, Céline, showing how a psychoanalytic theory can be applied to literature.

—— (1981) *Le langage, cet inconnu*. Paris: Éditions du Seuil. (English version, 1989, *Language, the Unknown: An Initiation into Linguistics*, trans. Anne Menke, New York: Columbia University Press.)

This is a little known book of Kristeva's, namely because of its genre: a textbook about linguistics. Rather than profess her own linguistic theory directly, Kristeva offers the student in linguistics a Kristevan account of the discipline, giving a detailed account of the history of semiotics and a multicultural history of the study of language. In its own right, this is a useful introduction to linguistics, especially for the student who wants to see what is pertinent in the history of linguistics for those doing literary theory today.

—— (1983) *Histoires d'amour*. Paris: Éditions Denoël. (English version, 1987, *Tales of Love*, trans. Leon S. Roudiez, New York: Columbia University Press.)

This book can be grouped with *Powers of Horror* and *Black Sun*; all make up a trilogy of Kristeva's psychoanalytic writings of the 1980s. *Tales of Love*, as the name indicates, focuses on the amorous emotion. In addition to a psychoanalytic account, Kristeva draws on philosophy, religion, and literature, with essays on Don Juan, Romeo and Juliet, Baudelaire, and Stendhal.

—— (1985) *Au commencement était l'amour*. Paris: Hachette. (English version, 1987, *In the Beginning Was Love: Psychoanalysis and Faith*, trans. Arthur Goldhammer, New York: Columbia University Press.)

In this very slim volume, based upon a series of lectures, Kristeva shows how love is central to both psychoanalysis and religion. This is a lovely little book, but not one of Kristeva's more central texts.

—— (1986) *The Kristeva Reader*, ed. Toril Moi. New York: Columbia University Press.

This is a good collection of Kristeva's early essays, some drawn from larger works and others that were originally stand-alone papers. Moi introduces each essay with a careful and useful synopsis. The thirteen essays are divided into two groups: one on linguistics, semiotics, and textuality; and the other on women, psychoanalysis, and politics.

—— (1987) *Soleil noir: Depression et mélancolie*. Paris: Gallimard. (English version, 1989, *Black Sun: Depression and Melancholia*, trans. Leon S. Roudiez, New York: Columbia University Press.)

A beautiful but difficult book, *Black Sun* gives a psychoanalytic take on depression and melancholia. In the first part of the book Kristeva gives her own novel account of a kind of depression often neglected by psychoanalysts: the kind that renders the subject hardly capable of or interested in speaking. Such subjects may not be the best candidates for psychoanalysis, but Kristeva shows the importance of tending to the way that moods and affects can be deployed – with some success – in literary and artistic creation. As examples, she takes the case of some of her women patients, of the artist, Hans Holbein the Younger (1497–1543); of the poet, Gérard de Nerval (discussed in Chapter 4 of this volume); and of the authors, Fyodor Dostoevsky (1821–1881) and Marguerite Duras (1914–1996).

—— (1989) *Étrangers à nous-mêmes*. Paris: Fayard. (English version, 1991, *Strangers to Ourselves*, trans. Leon S. Roudiez, New York: Columbia University Press.)

My favorite part of this book is the first chapter, "Toccata and Fugue for the Foreigner," a rare first-person account of Kristeva's experience as a foreigner in France. She writes of the visceral experience of being a stranger in the midst of others; of being treated as strange, even abject; of having to break off from one's own mother/mother tongue. I once handed this chapter to my mother, a Greek living in the United

States, and she came back in tears. On a more politico-theoretical note, the final chapter offers a glimpse of what a truly cosmopolitan community might be like, of how we can embrace the foreigner within each of us (our own unconscious) as a way toward accepting the foreigners in our midst. This is a very powerful book.

—— (1993) *Les nouvelles maladies de l'âme*. Paris: Fayard. (English version, 1995, *New Maladies of the Soul*, trans. Ross Guberman, New York: Columbia University Press.)

As I discussed in Chapter 7, this volume is central to understanding Kristeva's account of how contemporary society has created new kinds of neuroses. Many of these revolve around a loss of psychic space, the "inner garden" of the soul. In this volume, Kristeva shows the danger that contemporary addictions and distractions pose for the possibility of being a fully developed human being. Interestingly, Kristeva draws on a number of tantalizing case studies from her own psychoanalytic practice.

—— (1993) *Nations without Nationalism*, partly translated by Leon S. Roudiez from *Lettre ouverte à Harlem Désir*. New York: Columbia University Press.

Described in my conclusion, this book affords a look at Kristeva's more recent forays into writing about politics. For the most part, it is quite accessible, though the reader would do well to know in advance a bit about recent political events in France.

—— (1996) *Julia Kristeva Interviews*, ed. Ross Mitchell Guberman. New York: Columbia University Press.

This book of interviews, conducted by two dozen different interviewers over the course of twenty-odd years, provides an excellent entry into Kristeva's thinking. Thanks to the conversational tone and the question-and-answer format, readers get an accessible and personal glimpse of Kristeva's thinking behind her writing. Moreover, at the center of the volume is a photo essay, with nearly twenty photos of Kristeva, spanning her infancy, her years in Paris in the 1960s, and her maturation as a leading European cultural critic and analyst.

—— (1996) *Sens et non-sens de la révolte: Pouvoirs et limites de la psychanalyse I*. Paris: Fayard. (English version, 2000, *The Sense and Non-sense of Revolt: The Powers and Limits of Psychoanalysis Vol. 1*, trans. Jeanine Herman, New York: Columbia University Press.)

This book is the first of several that Kristeva has recently written on the topic of revolt, discussed in detail in Chapter 7 of this book.

—— (1997) *The Portable Kristeva*, ed. Kelly Oliver. New York: Columbia University Press.

While this book was published a decade after Toril Moi's *Kristeva Reader*, it covers some of the same ground, including excerpts from *Revolution in Poetic Language* and the essays "Women's Time" and "Stabat Mater." It does, however, provide a more systematic representation of Kristeva's major theoretical texts, with big chunks of *Desire in Language*, *Tales of Love*, *Black Sun*, *New Maladies of the Soul*, *Powers of Horror*, and *Strangers to Ourselves* (including my favorite chapter from that volume). Moreover, this volume includes a wonderful but little known autobiographical essay that Kristeva wrote for the *New York Literary Forum* in 1984, "My Memory's Hyperbole."

—— (1997) *La révolte intime: Pouvoirs et limites de la psychanalyse II*. Paris: Fayard. (English version, 2002, *Intimate Revolt*, trans. Jeanine Herman, New York: Columbia University Press.)

—— (1998) *L'avenir d'une révolte*. Paris: Calmann-Levy. (English version, 2002, *Intimate Revolt*, trans. Jeanine Herman, New York: Columbia University Press.)

The English text, *Intimate Revolt*, contains two parts: the first is a translation of *La révolte intime* and the second a translation of *L'avenir d'une révolte*. Part 1, "Intimate Revolt," is the second volume of her series on the powers and limits of psychoanalysis. It explores the necessity of revolt for the experience of intimacy and the vitality of interior life, focusing on the works of the modern writers, Jean-Paul Sartre, Roland Barthes, and Louis Aragon. Part 2, "The Future of Revolt," contains three of her more personal essays, one on her interest in psychoanalysis, another on the situation of a foreigner and language, and a third on her relationship toward, and feelings about, America.

—— (1998) *Contre la dépression nationale: Entretien avec Philippe Petit*. Paris: Les Editions Textuel. (English version, 2002, *Revolt, She Said*, ed. Sylvère Lotringer and trans. Brian O'Keeffe, Los Angeles and New York: Semiotext(e).)

This small and friendly book of interviews with Julia Kristeva, conducted by the writers, Philippe Petit and Rubén Gallo, and the artist, Rainer Ganahl, takes up Kristeva's claim that "happiness only exists at the price of revolt." Coming on the heels of her three recent books on the topic of revolt, this book of interviews offers a useful and accessible introduction into why Kristeva thinks revolt is so vital.

—— (1999) *Le génie feminine, tome I: Hannah Arendt*. Paris: Librairie Arthème Fayard. (English version, 2001, *Hannah Arendt*, trans. Ross Guberman, New York: Columbia University Press.)

Hannah Arendt is the first volume of Kristeva's trilogy, *Female Genius: Life, Madness, Words – Hannah Arendt, Melanie Klein, Colette*. The first two volumes on the political philosopher, Hannah Arendt (1906–1975), and the pioneering psychoanalyst, Melanie Klein (1882–1960), are now translated into English; the third, on the French writer, Sidonie Gabrielle Colette (1873–1954), has yet to be translated. Kristeva's genre in these texts, despite the trilogy's title, is not quite that of intellectual biography, but it is more of an overview of the major themes in her subjects' works. The Arendt volume is comprised of three long chapters: "Life as a Narrative," "Superfluous Humanity," and "Thinking, Willing, and Judging," each covering a chronological span of Arendt's writings. Oddly, to have been written by an author who is such a powerful philosopher in her own right, these pages contain only the most subtle traces of Kristeva's own themes. Especially in the first two chapters, reading Kristeva on Arendt is like reading Arendt at a mere step's remove. Most of the passages seem to paraphrase Arendt. But in the remove of this one step the careful reader can find Kristeva's mark. Kristeva's major lament seems to be that, in denying the political import of psychic life, Arendt dismissed any need for a discourse of this life, that is, for psychoanalysis. Still, on the whole, the book shows Kristeva's profound respect for Arendt's thought and ample reason for readers to renew their appreciation for Arendt's works.

—— (2000) *Le génie feminine, tome II: Melanie Klein*. Paris: Librairie Arthème Fayard. (English version, 2001, *Melanie Klein*, trans. Ross Guberman, New York: Columbia University Press.)

This second volume of Kristeva's trilogy, *Female Genius: Life, Madness, Words – Hannah Arendt, Melanie Klein, Colette* takes up the life of the trailblazing psychoanalyst, Melanie Klein. Kristeva recounts how Klein, an unhappy wife and mother without any advance degree, went into analysis and became an analyst herself, eventually breaking ranks with Sigmund Freud to forge her own theory of the importance of the role of the mother in an infant's development, all the while remaining loyal to Freud's fundamental theory. Klein helped develop psychoanalytic approaches toward children, autism, and psychosis. She also helped develop a school known as object-relations theory, which argues that relationships are central in developing the psyche and not, as the classical school held, instincts. In addition to writing an intellectual biography of Klein, in this volume Kristeva gives the reader a history of psychoanalysis in the twentieth century.

—— (2000) *Crisis of the European Subject*, trans. Susan Fairfield. New York: Other Press.

This small book has four parts: (1) an excerpt from one of her books on Hannah Arendt; (2) an essay on the meaning of legal equality for women; (3) her reflections on the problem of religion in attempts to unify Europe; and (4) a personal essay on her relationship with her native land, Bulgaria, and native language, Bulgarian. As diverse as the elements are, the unifying theme is the intersection of culture and politics; ultimately, the possibility of carrying on any kind of productive politics in the contemporary world.

—— (2001) *Hannah Arendt: Life is a Narrative*, trans. Frank Collins. Toronto: University of Toronto Press.

Continuing her interest in the life and work of Hannah Arendt, Kristeva further explores the way Arendt integrated the life of the mind and political engagement. This volume is based upon a series of lectures that Kristeva gave at the University of Toronto.

WORKS ON JULIA KRISTEVA

Butler, Judith (1990) *Gender Trouble: Feminism and the Subversion of Identity*. New York and London: Routledge.

Butler's critical assessment of Kristeva's work, in the chapter, "The Body Politics of Julia Kristeva," has also been collected in Kelly Oliver's anthology, *Ethics, Politics, and Difference in Julia Kristeva's Writing*. Butler takes issue with the way theorists, Kristeva included, attempt to "fix" gender identities. Butler thinks Kristeva does this by way of tying the semiotic mode of signification to the feminine, maternal body.

Chanter, Tina and Ewa Ziarek (eds) (forthcoming) *Between Revolt and Melancholia: The Unstable Boundaries of Kristeva's Polis*. Albany: State University of New York Press.

This collection of original essays focuses on Julia Kristeva's most recent work. The essays, written by a range of Kristeva scholars in England and the United States, draw out the implications of Kristeva's writings on the concept of revolt and the question of the stranger, as well as on issues of race, nation, and community. They also address Kristeva's continuing interests in abjection, melancholia, narcissism, and aesthetics. As a whole, the volume provides the most current assessment of Kristeva's work by Kristeva scholars to date.

Crownfield, David (ed.) (1992) *Body/Text in Julia Kristeva: Religion, Women, and Psychoanalysis*. Albany: State University of New York Press.

Even the agnostically inclined will find this volume interesting. The editor provides a thorough introduction to Kristeva and her work, clearing up some misperceptions about her biography and highlighting the importance of Bakhtin in her intellectual development (which I briefly discussed in "Why Kristeva?"). Throughout the anthology, the editor interposes sets of questions and themes that the readings raise, primarily with respect to ethics, religion, language, and the experience of Kristeva's subject in process/on trial.

Fletcher, John and Andrew Benjamin (1990) *Abjection, Melancholia and Love: The Work of Julia Kristeva*. London: Routledge.

A bit dated now but still an excellent resource, this volume is a publication of eight papers presented at a 1987 University of Warwick conference on Kristeva, including one by Kristeva herself, plus three papers written subsequently. The papers address two sets of themes: one on art, literature, and representation, and another on feminism and philosophical issues.

Fraser, Nancy and Sandra Lee Bartky (eds) (1992) *Revaluing French Feminism: Critical Essays on Difference, Agency, and Culture*. Bloomington: Indiana University Press.

In this collection of essays, several prominent Anglo-American feminist philosophers assess the feminism of the work of four key French feminists: Simone de Beauvoir, Sarah Kofman, Luce Irigaray, and Julia Kristeva. (One wonders what happened to Hélène Cixous, usually included with Irigaray and Kristeva under the heading, "the French feminists.") The last four essays in this volume specifically address Julia Kristeva's work, all for the most part quite critically. Judith Butler's essay, drawn from her book, *Gender Trouble* (1990), makes a compelling case that Kristeva does a poor job of psychoanalyzing lesbianism, though Butler's analysis of Kristeva's semiotic/symbolic dichotomy has its own problems. See Kelly Oliver's rebuttal in *Reading Kristeva: Unraveling the Double-bind* (1993). Nancy Fraser's essay, "The Uses and Abuses of French Discourse Theories for Feminist Politics," is the most scathing one in the volume – perhaps because of its oversimplifications. See my rebuttal to Fraser in *Habermas, Kristeva, and Citizenship* (2000).

Grosz, Elizabeth (1989) *Sexual Subversions: Three French Feminists*. London: Allen & Unwin.

This book focuses on the French feminists, Julia Kristeva, Luce Irigaray, and Michèle Le Doeuff. Grosz's writing on Kristeva serves as a good introduction to her work.

Oliver, Kelly (ed.) (1993) *Ethics, Politics, and Difference in Julia Kristeva's Writing*. New York: Routledge.

This volume begins with an introduction by Kelly Oliver and brings together fourteen, mostly sympathetic, essays on Kristeva's work (though a critical essay by Judith Butler is reprinted again here). Most of the authors are "continental" feminist philosophers working in the Anglo-American world, so many share Kristeva's view of subjectivity and heterogeneity.

Oliver, Kelly (1993) *Reading Kristeva: Unraveling the Double-bind*. Bloomington: Indiana University Press.

This is a "must read" for anyone interested in a sustained, in-depth analysis and defense of Julia Kristeva's work. Interestingly, Oliver began her research critically, under the guidance of one of Kristeva's biggest critics (see above). But the more Oliver read of and on Kristeva, the more sympathetic she became. This shows in her point-by-point response to the various criticisms that have been leveled against Kristeva's theories.

WEB SITES

http://www.cddc.vt.edu/feminism/Kristeva.html

The text for this site was written by Kelly Oliver. It is brief and useful and includes a 1998 interview with Kristeva. It contains some links to other sites as well.

http://www.bailiwick.lib.uiowa.edu/wstudies/frenchfem.html

This has an extensive collection of Internet sources on the French feminists.

http://www.press.jhu.edu/books/hopkins_guide_to_literary_theory /julia_kristeva.html

This entry from the *Johns Hopkins Guide to Literary Theory and Criticism* is also written by Kelly Oliver. It makes good use of the Web's hypertext medium, providing links to related topics and figures.

http://www.nyartsmagazine.com/57/juliakristeva.html

This interview conducted with Kristeva in the Spring of 2001 focuses on Kristeva's views on "the feminine" and art. In it she also discusses the links between her interests in revolt, Arendt, and Colette.

WORKS CITED

Adams, Hazard and Leroy Searle (eds) (1986) *Critical Theory Since 1965*. Tallahasee: University Presses of Florida, Florida State University Press.

Ainley, Alison (1990) "The Ethics of Sexual Difference," in John Fletcher and Andrew Benjamin (eds) *Abjection, Melancholia and Love: The Work of Julia Kristeva*. London: Routledge.

Chanter, Tina (1993) "Kristeva's Politics of Change: Tracking Essentialism with the Help of a Sex/Gender Map," in Kelly Oliver (ed.) *Ethics, Politics, and Difference in Julia Kristeva's Writing*. New York: Routledge.

——— (2001) "Abject Images: Kristeva, Art, and Third Cinema," *Philosophy Today* 45(5), SPEP Supplement: 83–98.

Crownfield, David (ed.) (1992) *Body/Text in Julia Kristeva: Religion, Women, and Psychoanalysis*. Albany: State University of New York Press.

Debord, Guy (1983) *Society of the Spectacle*. Detroit: Black & Red.

Edwards, Peter J. (1999) "Gérard de Nerval," in Robert Beum (ed.) *Gale Group Database: Dictionary of Literary* Biography, Vol. 217: Nineteenth-century French Poets. A Bruccoli Clark Layman Book. The Gale Group, pp. 227–242. Available online at http://www.galenet.galegroup.com (no page numbers).

Fletcher, John, and Andrew Benjamin (eds) (1990) *Abjection, Melancholia and Love: The Work of Julia Kristeva*. London: Routledge.

Foster, Hal (1996) *The Return of the Real*. Cambridge, MA: MIT Press.

Fraser, Nancy (1992) "The Uses and Abuses of French Discourse Theories for Feminist Politics," in Nancy Fraser and Sandra Lee Bartky (eds) *Revaluing French Feminism: Critical Essays on Difference, Agency, and Culture*. Bloomington: Indiana University Press.

Fraser, Nancy, and Sandra Lee Bartky (eds) (1992) *Revaluing French Feminism: Critical Essays on Difference, Agency, and Culture*. Bloomington: Indiana University Press.

Freud, Sigmund [1919] (1953) "The Uncanny," in *Complete Works: Standard Edition*, vol. 17. London: Hogarth, pp. 217–252.

Gale Group's Literary Databases of Contemporary Authors (2003) Online. Available at http://www.galenet.com.

Guberman, Ross (ed.) (1996) *Julia Kristeva Interviews*. New York: Columbia University Press.

Hegel, G.W.F. (1997) *Phenomenology of Spirit*, trans. A.V. Miller. Oxford: Oxford University Press.

Hughes-Hallett, Lucy (1992) "Egghead Out of Her Shell," *The Independent* (London), 9 February 1992, The Sunday Review Page: 26.

Huntington, Patricia J. (1998) *Ecstatic Subjects, Utopia, and Recognition: Kristeva, Heidegger, Irigaray*. Albany: State University of New York Press.

Joyce, James (1986) *Ulysses: The Corrected Text*. New York: Vintage Books.

Krauss, Rosalind (1996) "*Informe* without Conclusion," *October* 78, Fall: 89–105.

Kristeva, Julia (1977) "Hérethique de l'amour," *Tel Quel* 74, Winter: 30–49.

—— (1980) *Desire in Language*, trans. Thomas Gora, Alice Jardine, and Leon S. Roudiez and ed. Leon S. Roudiez. New York: Columbia University Press.

—— (1981) "Women's Time," *Signs* 7(1), Autumn: 13–35. Translation of "Le temps des femmes," in *33/44 Cahiers de recherche de science des texts et documents*, 5, Winter 1979: 5–19.

—— (1982) *Powers of Horror: An Essay on Abjection*, trans. Leon S. Roudiez. New York: Columbia University Press.

—— (1984) *Revolution in Poetic Language*, trans. Leon S. Roudiez. New York: Columbia University Press.

—— (1986) *The Kristeva Reader*, ed. Toril Moi. New York: Columbia University Press.

—— (1987) *Tales of Love*, trans. Leon S. Roudiez. New York: Columbia University Press.

—— (1989a) *Black Sun: Depression and Melancholia*, trans. Leon S. Roudiez. New York: Columbia University Press.

—— (1989b) *Language, the Unknown: An Initiation into Linguistics*, trans. Anne Menke. New York: Columbia University Press.

—— (1991) *Strangers to Ourselves*, trans. Leon S. Roudiez. New York: Columbia University Press.

—— (1995) *New Maladies of the Soul*, trans. Ross Guberman. New York: Columbia University Press.

—— (1997) *The Portable Kristeva*, ed. Kelly Oliver. New York: Columbia University Press.

—— (2000) *The Sense and Non-sense of Revolt: The Powers and Limits of Psychoanalysis, Vol. 1*, trans. Jeanine Herman. New York: Columbia University Press.

Kuprel, Diana (2000) "In Defence of Human Singularity: Diana Kuprel Speaks with Julia Kristeva," *Canadian Review of Books* 28(8/9), January: 21–26.

Lacan, Jacques (1977) *Écrits: A Selection*, trans. Alan Sheridan. New York: W.W. Norton & Company.

Lechte, John (1990) "Art, Love, and Melancholy in the Work of Julia Kristeva," in John Fletcher and Andre Benjamin (eds) *Abjection, Melancholia, and Love*. London: Routledge.

—— (1997) *Fifty Contemporary Thinkers: From Structuralism to Post-modernity*. London: Routledge.

Lentricchia, Frank and Thomas McLaughlin (eds) (1990) *Critical Terms for Literary Study*. Chicago: University of Chicago Press.

McAfee, Noëlle (1993) "Abject Strangers: Toward an Ethics of Respect" in Kelly Oliver (ed.) *Ethics, Politics, and Difference in Julia Kristeva's Writing*. New York: Routledge.

—— (2000a) "Resisting Essence: Kristeva's Process Philosophy," *Philosophy Today* 44, SPEP Supplement: 77–83.

—— (2000b) *Habermas, Kristeva, and Citizenship*. Ithaca, NY: Cornell University Press.

Moi, Toril (1985) *Sexual/Textual Politics: Feminist Literary Theory*. London and New York: Routledge.

Moruzzi, Norma Claire (2000) *Speaking Through the Mask: Hannah Arendt and the Politics of Social Identity*. Ithaca, NY: Cornell University Press.

Nerval, Gérard de (1973) [1854] "El Desdichado," in *Les chimères*. London: Athlone Press.

Oliver, Kelly (1993) *Reading Kristeva: Unraveling the Double-bind*. Bloomington: Indiana University Press.

—— (ed.) (1993a) *Ethics, Politics, and Difference in Julia Kristeva's Writing*. New York: Routledge.

—— (1997) "Introduction," in Kelly Oliver (ed.) *The Portable Kristeva*. New York: Columbia University Press.

Plato (2000) *Timaeus*, trans. Donald J. Zeyl. Indianapolis: Hackett Publishing.

Rycroft, Charles (1968) *A Critical Dictionary of Psychoanalysis*. New York: Penguin.

Silverman, Kaja (1991) "Dis-Embodying the Female Voice," in Patricia Erens (ed.) *Issues in Feminist Film Criticism*. Bloomington: Indiana University Press, pp. 309–327.

Smith, Anna (1996) *Julia Kristeva: Readings of Exile and Estrangement*. New York: St Martin's Press.

Weir, Allison (1996) *Sacrificial Logics: Feminist Theory and the Critique of Identity*. New York and London: Routledge.

Ziarek, Ewa (1995) "The Uncanny Style of Kristeva's Critique of Nationalism, "*Postmodern Culture* 5(2), January. Online. Available at http://jefferson.village.virginia.edu/pmc/text-only/issue.195/ziarek.195.

—— (2001) *An Ethics of Dissensus: Postmodernity, Feminism, and the Politics of Radical Democracy*. Stanford, CA: Stanford University Press.

INDEX

Note: **emboldened** page numbers indicate boxed text.